Sustainable Business Development

Managing Change in an International Context

Series Editors

This open access book series focuses on the key success factors for sustainable business transformation, including the efficient use of resources, the systematic consideration of relevant aspects and technologies of digitalization, and the involvement of all relevant stakeholders. Furthermore, it identifies risks and opportunities for businesses arising from the climate crisis and digitalization and explores solutions to prevent or minimize negative effects. The series takes a multi-faceted, multi-disciplinary approach by integrating economic, sustainable, and technological perspectives. It welcomes monographs and contributed volumes from senior and promising young scholars.

Gaël Brulé

Reducing the Environmental Impact of Healthcare Systems

Between Frugal Innovation and AI

Springer

Gaël Brulé
Geneva School of Health Sciences
Genève, Switzerland

ISSN 3004-9644 ISSN 3004-9652 (electronic)
Sustainable Business Development
ISBN 978-3-032-34888-3 ISBN 978-3-032-34889-0 (eBook)
https://doi.org/10.1007/978-3-032-34889-0

This work was supported by SNSF.

This Springer imprint is published by the registered company Springer Nature Switzerland AG
The registered company address is: Gewerbestrasse 11, 6330 Cham, Switzerland

Acknowledgments I am grateful to Geneva School of Health Sciences for freeing me some time to work on this project. I am indebted to Natacha Bossi and to the library of Geneva School of Health Sciences, who have helped tremendously in the bibliometric analyses. I must also thank Thomas Gibon for helping me providing the schemes on the materiality of the sector. Some of the reflections stemmed from discussions from engaged colleagues who cannot all be cited here. The author wishes to thank Hugues Jeannerat, Christian Abshagen, Johanna Sommer, Sylvain de Lucia and Swann Pichon for their reading and precious feedback, as well as to many colleagues with whom I had related discussions on the topic. Artificial Intelligence(Claude 4) was used for editing and rephrasing purposes. Any remaining error or mistake is the sole responsibility of the author.

This book was supported by the Swiss National Science Foundation (SNSF) under grant number 243432.

Competing Interests The author has no competing interests to declare that are relevant to the content of this manuscript.

About This Book

The millions of masks in the sea and the rivers have become a tragic symbol of the healthcare system in the COVID-19 era. First barriers in the face of the adversity, they have also become a lasting and visible mark of a system largely based on single-use. Although the contribution of waste to the overall impact of the healthcare sector is relatively small (ca 5-10% in terms of carbon footprint), they highlight the idea that the healthcare sector is at the same time saving lives and jeopardizing others via the degradation of ecosystems, thus going against its very mission of non-maleficence (*primum non nocere*). Healthcare (HC) systems collectively account for 5 % of the global carbon emissions. It is common to represent it by saying that if they were a country, they would be the fourth largest emitter.

Yet, in recent years, things have begun to shift, and initiatives deployed to reduce emissions within healthcare institutions are booming. New guidelines, protocols, and technologies are emerging across various contexts in an effort to reduce their environmental footprint, i. and to address the disconnect many healthcare professionals experience between what they signed up for (save lives) and the reality that healthcare systems may simultaneously harm others through environmental damage. In the Anthropocene, healthcare institutions and professionals often feel insufficiently prepared to assess their environmental impact and, more importantly, to identify effective ways to avoid, reduce, mitigate it. Lack of time, lack of resources, lack of imagination or lack of space to think new ways of providing care are part of the brakes to bring significant changes to daily practices. Although many actors, whether institutional or individual, recognize the need for change, the lack of practical tools, case studies together with bureaucratic constraints and the limited time often make such changes difficult to implement. Framed positively, many institutions and healthcare professionals are in demand to innovate toward more sustainable practices but do not know where to start. This is the *raison d'être* of this book. We provide responses to these needs by presenting various types of innovation that can help reduce the environmental impacts of healthcare systems. Readers will not find a "cookbook" for innovation in healthcare; rather, they will discover nine distinct forms of innovation that suggest possible directions, along with a critical examination of the dominant current pathway, technological innovation. The ambition of this book is to broaden the reader's perspective by offering reflections, ideas and tools to support change within healthcare institutions. To this end, this book brings together different conceptual frameworks and case studies, as well as a proposed grammar of innovation. Below, we briefly present what are the core tenets of the book.

The contribution of this book is threefold. First, it proposes a grammar of innovations that can be used to understand how different forms of innovation affect the healthcare sector. Second, it analyses the indicators used to measure both environmental impact and innovation. Finally, it critically evaluates the existing literature on innovation in the healthcare sector based on this framework. At present, existing classifications of innovations whether within or beyond the healthcare sector do not adequately capture the variety of tools available. Therefore, efforts are often concentrated on two or three subtypes of innovation rather than on the full spectrum of the 9 forms of innovation. This is due to a number of biases (intervention bias, technological preferences) which tend to filter out other forms of innovation which may be much more promising in terms of reducing environmental impacts. By proposing nine distinct forms of innovation, this book extracts different innovations that are available either in the literature on health innovation or mostly outside. It thus offers a comprehensive portfolio of existing innovations that can be mobilized within the healthcare sector.

The Voice of the Environment

This book brings an environmental perspective to the debates on innovation in the healthcare sector. Therefore, it adopts a *strong sustainability* approach in which healthcare systems are not viewed as detached from ecosystems but rather as embedded within, made possible by them. The HC sector, like others, relies on finite resources (metals, fossil fuels, water, rare earths…) and impacts nature directly through climate change, pollution and biodiversity loss. It seeks to interrogate how healthcare systems can operate within planetary boundaries. While taking an environmental perspective, it also acknowledges that the quality of care must not be compromised.

Human Before All

This book posits that healthcare systems are deeply human, which means that environmental problems cannot be solved solely through efficiency gains or technological substitution. This is true for two reasons. The first one is environmental. When an environmental problem is tackled through technology, it tends to lead to a *rebound effect*, where the deflationary benefits of cost reduction are wiped out by an increase in new uses, thus overshadowing the initial benefits. For instance, as the efficiency of medical imaging in the UK doubled (i.e., the energy necessary for a scan was halved), the number of scans quadrupled, resulting in a doubling of total energy consumption. Rebound effects are a real warning for environmentalists and often a reality check for over-enthusiastic entrepreneurs or leaders who are prone to magical thinking. The second reason for getting away from solutions that are only technological is cultural. As technology-only is chosen, this leaves unchanged the maximalist imaginary (see final part on imaginaries) in place that leads to resource-intensive solutions.

Focus on Innovations

To avoid adding more negativity to a sector already where challenges are already numerous (stress, burnout, high turnover) and because efforts to reduce environmental impacts also bring their own share of discomfort, this book adopts a positive framing under the banner of innovation. Without refuting the urgency of changes, it seeks to look at it not as a "double burden" (Rivard et al., 2020), but as a double opportunity. However, as we have shown elsewhere, the most positive terms are particularly vulnerable to misconceptualization due to the power dynamics and imaginary struggle that they face (Brulé, 2024). In particular, it will question the current tendency to associate innovations with technology in order to open door to low-tech or organizational innovations. Many HC professionals are innovators on a daily basis but, like *Monsieur Jourdain* discovering he was speaking prose in Molière's *Le Bourgeois Gentillhomme*, they might not realize it. Part of this is a question of framing, as well as a tendency for a "winner-takes-all" dynamics in the representation of innovation, with the current assumption that innovation is only about Artificial Intelligence(AI) and Virtual Reality(VR). Innovations *can* be technological, no doubt. However, the spectrum of innovations is much richer and diversified once it is integrated into socio-cultural contexts. Also, while innovation *may* be based on technology, this also entails that in some other cases, renouncing technology may be the wisest choice. The fact that technology can be helpful means it is a tool, not a substitute for reasoning or imagination.

We have known since Schumpeter that innovation is a dual process, with dynamics of creation and dynamics of destruction intimately connected. Although this destruction is often considered from the perspective of previous technologies or the social fabrics it affects, it is also of major importance to examine the environmental degradation that innovations may lead to. This is particularly true as the dynamics of innovation are usually embedded in the long term. The *dilemma of control* (Collingridge, 1980) highlights the fact that in the early stages of development, innovation can still be redirected toward low-impact pathways, but their environmental consequences are not yet known. Conversely, once the environmental effects of certain innovations become known, they are already locked-in, making change very difficult. This is particularly true in the healthcare sector, where technologies, protocols and care pathways are usually in place for long time. The widespread adoption of single-use plastics in hospitals, initially promoted in the mid-twentieth century as hygienic, convenient, and cost-efficient, still embedded in protocols, procurement systems, and regulatory standards, is one example among many. Despite extensive evidence of their environmental burden, whether on the extractive side (upstream) or on the emissions (downstream), the structural dependence of healthcare on disposables makes transitions to circular alternatives very difficult. The promises of AI do not operate in a vacuum, but rely on data centers that consume large amounts of electricity and water for cooling.

Focus on Healthcare Delivery

While prevention and health promotion are essential topics, they are not the primary focus of this book. We fully acknowledge that they represent the most effective forms of care (we often remind our students that the greenest care is the care that is not needed) and offer the greatest potential for reducing environmental impacts (Marrauld et al., 2023). However, the chapters of this book do not address how to reduce disease incidence. Although healthcare represents only 10% of the overall health constituents (Shortell, 2013), it is where a significant share of environmental impacts occurs. This book instead responds to frequent questions we receive from healthcare professionals and institutions: what can we do, in our daily practice, to better reduce our environmental impacts?

Because this book is primarily intended for HC professionals and others interested in (re)thinking the healthcare system, it does not focus on architectural design, building energy systems, or hospital infrastructure planning such as Heating Ventilation Air Conditioning (HVAC) optimization or insulation. While these elements represent an important part of the healthcare system (20-25%), and although the environmental impact of healthcare buildings is a well-documented area of research (Eckelman & Sherman, 2016; Short & Al-Maiyah, 2009), such interventions typically fall within the domain of architects and engineers and lie largely outside the direct control of healthcare professionals and clinical teams. HVAC-related energy can be indirectly treated through the way healthcare professionals choose to deliver care rather than on the building itself. This will partly be treated in some forms of innovation (see, e.g., organizational innovation). Instead, this book focuses on what can be done within care delivery: clinical practices, social, and organizational dimensions, and the technologies that are adopted.

Meso Level

The healthcare system can be observed at various scales. At the macro level, policies shape the type of system that is adopted (e.g., reimbursement schemes, climate policies, carbon reduction targets, and R&D budgets). At the meso level, technologies are purchased, routines or/and clinical guidelines and practices are decided, norms are built and unbuilt, social fabrics meshed and unmeshed. At the micro scale, i.e. at the level of everyday practice, one can observe how choices and non-choices are made, how actions are carried out or neglected, within life trajectories that may be linear, disrupted or fragmented.

The book's primary analytic lens is the meso level, the organizational and institutional settings where care is planned, delivered, and regulated. Between macro-level forces (economic models, regulation, global supply chains) and micro-level behaviors (individual values and actions), the emphasis is on *situated innovations*, i.e., how groups of healthcare professionals, patients, managers, and policymakers engage with the challenge of environmental impact in a daily manner through clinical norms, professional routines and/or clinical practices, and infrastructure. Likewise, the geopolitical considerations of material and energy, such as the conditions of cobalt extraction in the Democratic Republic of the Congo, conflicts and wars for resources are not directly addressed in this book. The meso-level focus is an invitation to recognize the agency already present within healthcare systems, and seeks to make visible the practices, constraints, and imaginaries which shape their ecological footprint. This book examines how a wide range of sustainability-oriented solutions (frugal design, AI optimization, behavioral change, circular procurement) are being shaped, legitimized, or resisted within institutional contexts. The approach acknowledges that both macro-level governance targets and micro-level professional initiatives (e.g., green teams, clinical champions) influence these dynamics, but emphasizes that lasting transformation depends mostly on how these forces are negotiated within the operating (and operative) logic of healthcare systems.

Structure of the Book

We begin by establishing the historical background and methodological framework of this book by tracing the emergence of environmental awareness in healthcare (Chap. 1). After outlining the methodological frameworks used in this book (Chap. 2), we examine how the environmental impacts of the healthcare sector are assessed (Chap. 3). We then present the nine forms of innovation used in this book (Chap. 4). Finally, we discuss how literature views innovation in healthcare to reduce environmental burden and suggest axes of reflections in the future (Chap. 5).

References

Brulé, G. (2024). *Le coût environnemental du bonheur*. Éditions Épistémé. https://books.google.fr/books?hl=fr&lr=&id=k0sCEQAAQBAJ&oi=fnd&pg=PA7&dq=brul%C3%A9+le+cout+environnemental+du+bonheur&ots=5e3CC4Lrmk&sig=6TQ8sQblU4tFlzPT37Su4oI8ZLQ

Collingridge, D. (1980). The dilemma of control. *The Social Control of Technology*, 13–22.

Eckelman, M. J., & Sherman, J. (2016). Environmental impacts of the US health care system and effects on public health. *PloS One*, *11*(6), e0157014.

Rivard, L., Lehoux, P., & Miller, F. A. (2020). Double burden or single duty to care? Health innovators' perspectives on environmental considerations in health innovation design. *BMJ Innovations*, *6*, 4–9.

Marrauld, L., Egnell, M., Verneuil, B., & Rambaud, T. (2023). Soigner les patients tout en soignant la planète: Le bilan carbone du système de santé français et ses leviers de réduction. *Médecine Des Maladies Métaboliques*, *17*(4), 318–325

Short, C. A., & Al-Maiyah, S. (2009). Design strategy for low-energy ventilation and cooling of hospitals. *Building Research & Information*, *37*(3), 264–292. https://doi.org/10.1080/09613210902885156

Contents

Acronyms

AI	Artificial Intelligence
AMR	Antimicrobial Resistance
CO_2e	Carbon Dioxide Equivalent
CT	Computed Tomography
DALY	Disability-Adjusted Life Year
ERAS	Enhanced Recovery After Surgery
GHG	Greenhouse Gas
GWP100	Global Warming Potential over 100 years
HC	Healthcare
HIE	Health Information Exchange
HVAC	Heating, Ventilation, and Air Conditioning
ICU	Intensive Care Unit
ISO	International Organization for Standardization
LCA	Life Cycle Assessment
LMICs	Low- and Middle-Income Countries
MRI	Magnetic Resonance Imaging
NGOs	Non-governmental Organizations
NHS	National Health Service
OR	Operating Room
PPE	Personal Protective Equipment
SDGs	Sustainable Development Goals
UNEP	United Nations Environment Programme
VR	Virtual Reality
WHO	World Health Organization

Chapter 1
Historical Context

Abstract It is during the twentieth century, and especially its second half, that the multiple impacts the healthcare sector has on the environment have become substantial. A bibliometric analysis shows that the literature on the environmental impact of the sector has sparked interest later than other sectors such as the transport or the building sector. Looking at the last decades, one can observe that, after early isolated initiatives, the 2010s were the foundational decade whereas the 2020s represent the Great Acceleration period where sustainability really started to be a topic in a post-COVID-19 era.

Keywords Comparative analysis · Historical perspective · Awakening · Bibliometric analysis

In ancient Greece, and later in Rome, health was intimately connected to the seasons and the natural environment. Hippocrates emphasized the importance of "airs, waters, and places" and health was conceived as an equilibrium between the human body and the environment, in its natural dimension (air, water) but also its cultural one (diet, lifestyle, social customs). During the Middle Ages, the relation to the environment persisted within institutions as monastic medicine integrated natural remedies with communal care (Geadah, 2012). The Enlightenment marked a dramatic turn, as modern European cultures, in their effort to liberate rational thought from the influence of the medieval Christian Church, ended up isolating the human body from its context (Pietroni & Pietroni, 1996).[1] This intellectual rupture paved the way for deeper transformations from the nineteenth century onward, as steam engines and fossil fuels were reshaping the landscape, drawing populations from the countryside to the cities in what could look like a Turner painting. Modern public health and hygiene emerged in response to epidemics in the urban fabrics, with figures such

[1] Ironically, the Church had earlier performed a similar disjunction but in reverse, placing the care of the soul above the care of the body. In both cases, the result was a form of reductionism: medieval spirituality neglected the somatic, while modern biomedicine tends to overlook the existential and relational. It is frequent that pre-modern, modern, and post-modern use similar tools and end up being less different that they wish (Latour, 2012).

G. Brulé, *Reducing the Environmental Impact of Healthcare Systems*, Sustainable Business Development, https://doi.org/10.1007/978-3-032-34889-0_1

as Edwin Chadwick and John Snow often seen as central figures. At the same time, clinical medicine entered the era of specialization and sterility, based on the discoveries of Louis Pasteur, Joseph Lister and Robert Koch (Novick & Mays, 2005). The twentieth century saw a dramatic reconfiguration of the HC sector around a technological, biomedical, hospital-centered paradigm, following the Flexner Report (1910) and the Hill-Burton Act (1946) in the United States and the Beveridge Report in the United Kingdom (1942) (Cellucci et al., 2019; Shi & Singh, 2022).

These changes led to remarkable gains in population health. Life expectancy was around 35–40 years during the Middle ages, driven down by child mortality, poor health conditions, lack of knowledge in health in general (the miasma theory was dominant until Pasteur) and unpredictable yields in agriculture (Zeitoun, 2021). Since the middle of the twentieth century, global average life expectancy has risen from 45 years in 1950 to 72 years in 2022, with many high-income countries exceeding 80 years. Antibiotics alone are estimated to have saved tens of millions of lives worldwide since their introduction. Imaging technologies such as CT and MRI have made it possible to diagnose diseases in a radically new way. Intensive care units (ICUs) paved the way to survive injuries and sepsis. Not only have these technologies increased the *quantity of life*, but they also improved the *quality of life,* by enhancing the way chronic diseases (diabetes, hypertension, cancer) or disabilities (mobility loss, visions issues, dementia) are experienced by patients on a daily basis. In many ways, the story of the healthcare system is one of grandeur and triumph, especially when looking at it since the mid-nineteenth century.

However, as Homer and Virgil showed us, heroism is never unambiguous as every triumph carries a cost. The triumph of healthcare is no exception, and is in many ways Janus-headed. The very innovations that have improved longevity have normalized high-resource throughput as a clinical necessity. For decades, healthcare's own environmental impact was not questioned. Environmental protection, where it existed, was addressed externally, via sanitation departments, urban planning, or occupational health, not by questioning the ecological cost of medicine itself. It was (and it is) estimated that from a temporal and a spatial perspective, the benefits of healthcare were largely surpassing the costs.

This assumption was recently questioned. Today, healthcare's environmental impact is no longer invisible and as in other domains such as transportation, building or industry, but with a delay, the awareness of the impacts of the healthcare sector is growing. The *re*-consideration of the environment in the health sector is recent and apart from an important report from the World Health Organization focusing on Environmental Health (1994) and from isolated initiatives here and there, did not occur before the twenty-first century. Reports from the UK's NHS (2007) and organizations like Health Care Without Harm revealed that healthcare systems contribute to an amount ranging from 4 to 8% of national greenhouse gas emissions in many countries (Boyd et al., 2019; Naylor et al., 2020). At the same time, a landmark report from the Institute of Medicine(Health et al., 2011) challenged the sector's narrow focus on clinical performance and urged it to expand its definition of health outcomes to include environmental and social determinants. As we shall see throughout this book, *innovations* to reduce the environmental footprint of the healthcare system are blossoming in many hospitals, clinics, pharmacies, private practices. Healthcare professionals are triggering initiatives in many departments throughout the globe. Life cycle assessments, hospital carbon audits, green certifications, and new sustainability standards are emerging (Eckelman & Sherman, 2016; Sherman et al., 2019). At the moment at which these lines are written, the Geneva University Hospitals (HUG) became the first European hospitals to be awarded the Healthcare Sustainability Certification.

Yet this shift is only starting. As we shall see in the next chapter, the sector is in many ways less mature than other fields for cultural and structural reasons. Unlike other sectors, green certifications are only starting to be chased. Many healthcare institutions or professionals lack the language or tools to act toward a more sustainable healthcare system. There is a *lag* between the willingness-to-act and the possibilities to do so. Since COVID-19 in particular, sustainability has entered the daily narratives of HC institutions and workers. Seeing the amount of plastics and later realizing that this was only the tip of the iceberg of the environmental impacts, many HC workers felt that things were going *backwards*, that the impacts of the curing activities were preventing the Hippocratic duty "first do not harm". Many HC workers reported feeling sick when seeing the amount of wastes generated by some services.

How did the environmental narrative enter the healthcare sector? Without going into each detail, one can draw the main points that made that encounter possible. Historians would not necessarily agree on who pioneered ecology before the twentieth century. John Ray, Carl Linnaeus or Georges Louis Leclerc de Buffon for their taxonomy of plants, Alexander von Humboldt or later Antoine Rauch for linking climate, biodiversity and human activities, Ernst Haeckel for coining the term ecology. In more recent times, it is generally agreed that ecological awareness became a scientific, societal and political topic in the 1960s under the leadership of Rachel Carson and the scientists revolved around her (Eugene and Howard Odum, Garrett Hardin, Barry Commoner, Murray Bookchin to cite a few). She is seen as the leading figure paving the way for others to think in systems with her eye-opening books, *The Sea Around Us* (1951) and *Silent Spring* (1962). The former looked at the oceans as finite and vulnerable (and no longer as infinite and self-resorbing) whereas the latter documented the effects of anthropic activities and in particular on the trophic chain and the feedback loop it had on human health and is often cited as the bible of modern ecology. This book and Rachel Carson (physically) took position against the triumphant chemical industry of the time just a few years after the Swiss chemist Paul Hermann Müller had received, for his work on the promises of DDT, the Nobel Price of medicine. During the 1960s, her book and personal impulse aggregated civil, political and scientific forces for the first time into an emerging moment, the ecology ("the study of home").[2] The ecological movements have encountered downs (the oil crisis and the conservative government of the late 1970s early 80 s) and some ups (the Brundtland Commission and the Rio Earth Summit in the late 80 s-early 90 s).

---

[2] The term itself is generally attributed to the German biologist Ernst Haeckel who defined it as "the whole science of the relations of the organism to the environment".

They have relied on important actors (Denis and Donella Meadows, James Lovelock, André Gorz, Arne Naess, Vandana Shiva…) and have faced many opponents, especially in the private sector (petrochemistry, intensive agriculture, pharmaceutical industry, finance).

What is now known as sustainable development (or sustainability)[3] emerged from the Brundtland commission. Despite many objections that can be made to the term and the circumstances during which it was negotiated (Rist, 2014), it became a language that was used across different countries and different sectors. While the United States is the country in which the main authors started to push for ecological movements, environmental sustainability began shaping some major sectors well before others. In the transportation sector, grey literature was released on shifting from cars to public transport by the UITP (International Association of Public Transport),[4] anticipating the congestion effects and effects on the environment. This interest was later reinforced by the oil crises of the 1970s (1973, 1979) while public transportation was also seen as economically viable and necessary for security reasons. European cities in the Netherlands and Germany also influenced that movement. This was supported by visionary figures such as Amory Lovins, who pioneered systems thinking in energy-efficient transport (Lovins, 1974), Jan Gehl, who studied pedestrian-friendly urban design in Copenhagen (Gehl, 1971) or Ivan Illich who questioned speed-based mobility and advocated for human-scale transportation (Illich, 1974).

The interest in the housing sector appeared during the oil crises of the 1970s, which led to the development of energy-conservation measures and, eventually to the passive house movement in Germany in the 1980s. This also had to do with leading figures such as Hassan Fathy, who promoted vernacular, low-impact architecture in the early 1970s (Fathy, 2010), Edward Mazria, and Brenda and Robert Vale, who popularized the principles of passive-solar design (Mazria, 1979; Vale & Vale, 1975). Later, physicist Wolfgang Feist developed with Bo Adamson a concept of *Passivhaus* in Darmstadt in 1991 in order to erect a standard of ultra-low energy buildings. In the Kyoto protocol, the building sector was recognized as a major CO_2 contributor. Books layed out good practices (Passive House Planning Package 1998). Standards of efficient buildings such as BREEAM (1990) or LEED (1998) were erected to plan energy-saving buildings at a larger, more replicable scale. In the EU Energy Performance of Buildings Directive (2002), energy performance was demanded.

In the industry sector, historic accidents such as the Great Smog of London (1952), the accident of Minamata in Japan (1958), Seveso (1976), the Bhopal disaster in India (1984), the Chernobyl nuclear accident (1986), the Exxon Valdez oil spill (1989) led to institutional responses such as the creation of the "polluter payer" principle, the Clean Air Act, the creation of the Environmental Protection Agency or the Clean Water Act. The discovery of the ozone hole led to the Montreal Protocol (1987).

---

[3] To read about the differences between the terms in English (Ruggerio, 2021) and in French (Fragnière, 2022).

[4] "Public transport within the framework of urban general traffic plans" from their 34th International Congress in Copenhagen (1961), and "Regional organisation of transport and urban development" from their 38th International Congress in London (1969).

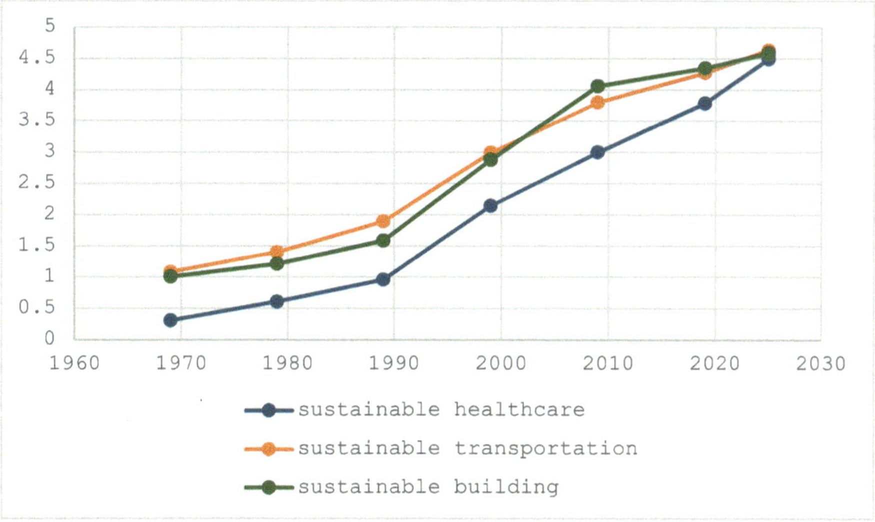

Fig. 1.1 Number of publications per field (logarithmic scale). Google Scholar searches for "sustainable [sector]" by decade

By the early 2000s, most major economic sectors had established environmental performance indicators and dedicated institutional structures for managing their environmental impacts. All except the healthcare sector. When taking a comparative lens, the late awakening of the healthcare sector is remarkable, especially when considering the goal of the sector: having people live longer. This cultural and institutional lag could be documented in many ways (policy analysis, archives) but academic traces seem to be a sensible way to observe differences because they reflect and shape institutional priorities. Other databases show similar results (see Appendix B) (Fig. 1.1).

It appears clearly that the scientific interest in sustainability in healthcare emerged after other sectors. The 10 publication landmark was achieved in the 1990s compared to the 1960s for transportation and building and the 10,000 landmark in the 2020s compared to 2000s for the building industry and 2010s for the transportation sector. But the recent dynamics behind sustainability in healthcare deserve a closer look as the speed of its catching up is remarkable. More articles have been published since COVID-19 pandemic than ever. As the contributions before the Brundtland Commission and Rio Conference are marginal in that sector, one can look at the development since 1990 in 4 different periods (Table 1.1).

It is also possible to observe the late interest in environmental matters by looking at the MeSH (Medical Subject Headings) terms. While "Quality of Health Care" entered medical terminology in 1968 and "Social Justice" in 1978, environmental concepts such as "recycling" appeared only in 2011, "Social Determinants of Health" in 2014. To date (early 2026), no MeSH terms yet exist for "sustainability", "planetary health", or "environmental impact of healthcare". This absence in medicine's standardized

Table 1.1 Scientific publications per decade

Period	Number of publications on sustainable healthcare	Key drivers
1990–1999	140	Early environmental awareness, waste management focus
2000–2009	998	Climate science emergence, NHS carbon footprint
2010–2019	6220	Paris agreement, Policy frameworks, terminology standardization
2020–2025	18,200	Climate emergency, COVID-19, Net Zero commitments

Data based on google scholar search for exact terms "sustainable healthcare" by publication year

vocabulary reflects what the American sociologist William Ogburn coined "cultural lag". While conceptual frameworks such as "Environmental Health" (1999) and "Environmental Pollution" (1974) entered medical vocabulary relatively early, more precise measures such as "Climate Change" and "Carbon Footprint" emerged later (respectively 2010 and 2011), despite scientific consensus emerging in the 1990s (see Appendix Table A.1).

The Silent Era (1990–1999)

After at least three decades of accumulation of scientific evidence in the field of environmental studies, the 90 s are undoubtedly its political moment following the Brundtland Commission and the Rio Conference. At the time, a large scientific-political front to fight the hole in the ozone layer through the ban of the Chlorofluorocarbons via the Montreal protocol. That is also the period at which the healthcare sector joined the movement, even from a distant perspective, with the creation of the term of *environmental health* by the WHO at the conference of Helsinki in 1994, the realization that incineration of medical waste was responsible for dioxin and mercury emissions (Pisters et al., 2017). But at the time, healthcare institutions are focused on clinical quality improvement, technological advancement, and cost containment (Fennell & Adams, 2011) with environmental considerations largely absent from strategic planning and operational management. Hospitals implemented basic waste segregation protocols to comply with new medical waste regulations (Davies & Lowe, 1999), but these measures are mostly framed in terms of law compliance and less so about environmental degradation.

The Awakening Period (2000–2009)

The first recognition of the environmental impacts of the healthcare system dates back to the 2000s. One groundbreaking moment comes in 2008 (updated in 2009) with the NHS carbon footprint report, conducted by the Sustainable Development Commission, which reveals that the British healthcare system accounts for an estimated 4–5% of the national greenhouse gas emissions (a figure that would later be revised to 6.3%). The novelty of the report resides not only in its findings but also in its methodology, applying the same analytical rigor to environmental accounting that healthcare uses for clinical and financial performance. For the first time, a major healthcare system had quantified its impact, perceiving new ways through which it was degrading the environment. However, as in other sectors, this early recognition remained confined to the pioneers of the field. The initiatives during that period remained largely isolated and ignored by the vast majority of healthcare professionals and institutions (and countries).

The Foundational Decade (2010–2019)

The 2010s represent a crucial period for healthcare sustainability. The Centre for Sustainable Healthcare (CSH), established earlier (in 2008), develops during this period a model of "sustainable clinical practice" based on four principles: prevention, patient self-care, lean service delivery, and the use of low-carbon alternatives. This approach, combining clinical quality improvement with environmental impact reduction shows that environmental protection must not necessarily be done at the expense of healthcare delivery. Organizations such as *Health Care Without Harm* and the *Global Green and Healthy Hospitals* network begin coordinating efforts across continents to document and compare the reduction of emissions in healthcare systems. By 2019, the network represented over 1,000 hospitals across 34 countries. The message of the IPCC report to cut its global emissions by 45% by 2030 to avoid catastrophic climate change was integrated by healthcare leaders. Unlike previous climate assessments that focused primarily on energy and transport, the 2018 report explicitly called for emissions reductions across all sectors of the economy, placing healthcare as an actor of decarbonization and environmental impact mitigation. All this is reinforced by emerging awareness from the youth around figures such as Greta Thunberg and more frequent heatwaves. In parallel, this period sees the development of academic research infrastructure for healthcare sustainability. The Lancet begins publishing occasional papers on health and climate change. The British Medical Association declares a climate emergency in 2019, followed quickly by medical associations worldwide.

The Great Acceleration (2020–2025)

The 2020s represent the period of mainstream adoption of sustainability within the healthcare sector. Although one could think environmental sustainability would be de-prioritized during the COVID-19 pandemic, the crisis also saw paradoxical accelerations of interest in sustainability within healthcare systems by exposing healthcare's deep dependence on complex global supply chains and single-use materials (hospitals reported waste increases of 20–30% during peak pandemic periods (World Health Organization, 2022). Medical students and young healthcare workers began organizing strikes and protests, demanding that their institutions better integrate environmental sciences, which became the case with the integration of curricula of environmental health (Pfarrwaller et al., 2024). The field of environmental health has seen a lot of improvement during the last years with key contributions (Braithwaite et al., 2024; Haines et al., 2017).

References

Boyd, R., Ashby, B., & Steele, K. (2019). Healthcare without harm. In *Healthcare's climate footprint–how the health sector contributes to the global climate crisis and opportunities for action* (Vol. 8).

Braithwaite, J., Smith, C. L., Leask, E., Wijekulasuriya, S., Brooke-Cowden, K., Fisher, G., Patel, R., Pagano, L., Rahimi-Ardabili, H., Spanos, S., Rojas, C., Partington, A., McQuillan, E., Dammery, G., Carrigan, A., Ehrenfeld, L., Coiera, E., Westbrook, J., & Zurynski, Y. (2024). Strategies and tactics to reduce the impact of healthcare on climate change: Systematic review. *BMJ, 387*, Article e081284. https://doi.org/10.1136/bmj-2024-081284

Cellucci, L. W., Meacham, M. R., & Farnsworth, T. J. (2019). *Essentials of healthcare management: Cases, concepts, and skills*. Health Administration Press (HAP). https://services.just.edu.jo/CourseQA/Uploads/Syllabus/147910.pdf

Davies, T., & Lowe, A. I. (1999). Environmental implications of the Health care service sector. *Discussion Papers, Discussion Papers*, Article 10857. https://ideas.repec.org//p/ags/rffdps/10857.html

Eckelman, M. J., & Sherman, J. (2016). Environmental impacts of the US health care system and effects on public health. *PLoS ONE, 11*(6), Article e0157014.

Fathy, H. (2010). *Architecture for the poor: An experiment in rural Egypt*. University of Chicago press. https://books.google.fr/books?hl=fr&lr=&id=KhrHzE5yOOkC&oi=fnd&pg=PR5&dq=Architecture+for+the+Poor+(1973)+&ots=DbGszkezbC&sig=c-HAYLXz8NO6HFFbbhQNYPuYOcU

Fennell, M. L., & Adams, C. M. (2011). U.S. Health-Care Organizations: Complexity, turbulence, and multilevel change. *Annual Review of Sociology, 37*(1), 205–219. https://doi.org/10.1146/annurev.soc.012809.102612

Fragnière, A. (2022). 2. Petit lexique commenté de la durabilité. In *Santé et environnement* (pp. 45–56). Médecine & Hygiène. https://shs.cairn.info/article/MH_SENN_2022_01_0045

Geadah, R.-R. (2012). A survey of the progress of care: Historical and ethical aspects of relations between health professionals and patients. *Recherche En Soins Infirmiers, 109*(2), 16–32.

Gehl, J. (1971). Life between buildings: Using public space Copenhagen. *Dan. Arch.*

Health, B. on P., Practice, P. H., & Health, C. on P. H. S. to I. (2011). *For the public's health: The role of measurement in action and accountability*. National Academies Press. https://books.google.fr/books?hl=fr&lr=&id=H00XT2d51jYC&oi=fnd&pg=PR1&dq=%E2%80%A2%09IOM+(Institute+of+Medicine).+(2011).+For+the+Public%E2%80%99s+Health:+The+Role+of+Measurement+in+Action+and+Accountability.+&ots=h_55nUdlJm&sig=QxGosDq-LN2ooxpa9_jItSMGuvQ

Haines, D. A., Saravanabhavan, G., Werry, K., & Khoury, C. (2017). An overview of human biomonitoring of environmental chemicals in the Canadian Health Measures Survey: 2007–2019. *International Journal of Hygiene and Environmental Health, 220*(2), 13–28.

Illich, I. (1974). *Energy and equity* (Vol. 6). Harper & Row New York. http://ww.w.ridemybike.org/energyandequity.pdf

Latour, B. (2012). *We have never been modern.* Harvard University Press. https://books.google.fr/books?hl=fr&lr=&id=xbnK8NzMsm4C&oi=fnd&pg=PP11&dq=latour+modern+never&ots=_VjLenv4Wd&sig=GnXulcZTnZPEOIsVX5hnFDMs204

Lovins, A. B. (1974). The case for long-term planning. *Bulletin of the Atomic Scientists, 30*(6), 38–50. https://doi.org/10.1080/00963402.1974.11458130

Mazria, E. (1979). *Passive solar energy book.* https://www.osti.gov/biblio/5473955

Naylor, C., Alderwick, H., & Honeyman, M. (2020). *Acute hospitals and integrated care: From hospitals to health systems: King's Fund; 2015.*

Novick, L. F., & Mays, G. P. (2005). *Public health administration: Principles for population-based management.* Jones & Bartlett Learning. https://books.google.fr/books?hl=fr&lr=&id=bFBPMcQe6ogC&oi=fnd&pg=PR13&dq=%E2%80%A2%09Novick,+L.+F.,+%26+Mays,+G.+P.+(2014).+Public+Health+Administration:+Principles+for+Population-Based+Management.&ots=iI9O0qlV9a&sig=5Q_Bsmf7EKrfRzQ-yGQ0ovGxhDQ

Pfarrwaller, E., Prasad, P., De Lucia, S., & Haller, D. M. (2024). Feasibility and acceptability of a primary care mentoring programme for undergraduate students. *Education for Primary Care, 35*(3–4), 101–108. https://doi.org/10.1080/14739879.2024.2330999

Pietroni, P., & Pietroni, C. (1996). Innovation in community care and primary health: The Marylebone experiment. *(No Title).* https://cir.nii.ac.jp/crid/1130000794209891968

Pisters, P., Bien, B., Dankner, S., Rubinstein, E., & Sheriff, F. (2017). Supporting hospital renewal through strategic environmental sustainability programs. *Healthcare Management Forum, 30*(2), 79–83. https://doi.org/10.1177/0840470416674481

Rist, G. (2014). *The history of development: From western origins to global faith.* Bloomsbury Publishing. https://books.google.fr/books?hl=fr&lr=&id=vv00EAAAQBAJ&oi=fnd&pg=PP1&dq=gilbert+rist+development&ots=n5p9H7eh7l&sig=xrp2Z-HnBCbSi8HUwJanacYWwvk

Ruggerio, C. A. (2021). Sustainability and sustainable development: A review of principles and definitions. *Science of the Total Environment, 786*, Article 147481.

Sherman, J. D., MacNeill, A., & Thiel, C. (2019). Reducing pollution from the health care industry. *JAMA, 322*(11), 1043–1044.

Shi, L., & Singh, D. A. (2022). *Essentials of the US health care system.* Jones & Bartlett Learning. https://books.google.fr/books?hl=fr&lr=&id=c890EAAAQBAJ&oi=fnd&pg=PP1&dq=%E2%80%A2%09Shi,+L.,+%26+Singh,+D.+A.+(2014).+Essentials+of+the+U.S.+Health+Care+System.&ots=tEBNfgt6kz&sig=mECzxuUSERT4MHtf7QldgGOkmGE

Vale, B., & Vale, R. J. D. (1975). The Autonomous House: Design and planning for self-sufficiency. *(No Title).* https://cir.nii.ac.jp/crid/1130000795295433344

World Health Organization, W. H. (2022). *Global analysis of healthcare waste in the context of COVID-19: Status, impacts and recommendations.* World Health Organization. https://books.google.fr/books?hl=fr&lr=&id=TngOEQAAQBAJ&oi=fnd&pg=PR11&dq=Global+analysis+of+health+care+waste+in+the+context+of+COVID-19&ots=W3wQtsLhOZ&sig=RP_hXI8nMtoDM9W2keDbyKbsLK4

Zeitoun, J.-D. (2021). *La Grande Extension. Histoire de la santé humaine.* Denoël.

Chapter 2
Methods

Abstract This chapter provides the multi-method framework used to examine the environmental landscape of healthcare innovation, drawing on three complementary approaches. The first one is the bibliometric analysis of the existing literature (PubMed, OpenAlex, and Google Scholar), revealing areas of thematic density and existing gaps. The second method is a material perspective, quantifying the elemental composition and material footprint of healthcare systems or selected medical devices. The third method draws on direct observation at two events to classify innovations according to a three-tier framework (high-tech, mid-tech, and low-tech).

Bibliometric Analysis

In order to observe how the literature on innovation in healthcare, in particular vis-à-vis sustainability, is constituted, stratified and to see how it evolves, a bibliometric analysis was performed. This method offers a helicopter view of a research landscape, through the maping of key themes and actors (Kumar, 2025). This type of analysis has advantages that were demonstrated elsewhere (Hemmingsen et al., 2023). It makes it possible to observe where the literature is dense and where it presents gaps, to track research trends over time, in different countries, to compare specific areas of a given field and to observe the profile of authors and institutions. It is a frugal way of conducting research by tapping into what is already here. It also has some limits. First, boundaries are often blurrier than researchers would like and articles frequently span multiple themes. Second, it lacks a qualitative dimension. Some articles might be counted but offer very different degrees of insight. It must thus be completed by a deep reading of key articles. Third, it has a "winner" bias in the sense that only the ones that write are being documented. It is crucial to observe not only the documented landscapes but also the gaps and the silences of the field. The main source of information used was PubMed for its direct concern of the biomedical field, complemented where relevant by OpenAlex and Google Scholar, the former for its span and depth across disciplines, the latter for its access to grey literature.

G. Brulé, *Reducing the Environmental Impact of Healthcare Systems*, Sustainable Business Development, https://doi.org/10.1007/978-3-032-34889-0_2

Material Footprint

In a *material footprint analysis*, we quantified healthcare systems' resource use using databases such as EXIOBASE, which is a multiregional, input-output database in open access. It is based on a top-down approach where aggregate impacts at the global level are disaggregated to a specific product or service.

We have also used an *elemental count*, which we define as the number of chemical elements likely present and/or necessary in a medical device, which enables us to present an indicator of complexity which is largely ignored. This is, however, at the core of sustainable considerations, since products incorporating more elements are more dependent on some materials which are sometimes hard to obtain, harder to recycle, a phenomenon known as "material criticality" (Graedel et al., 2015). Exact compositions vary by manufacturer and model and are not known precisely, so the elemental counts we present here represent what is available in the scientific literature, manufacture documentation and informed estimates based on typical material compositions for each device category.

Fieldwork

A last part of the work was to document specific events related to innovation. Data were collected at two events, the Innovation Days organized by the Geneva University Hospital in 2024 and Healthcare Week Luxembourg. During these two events, innovations were classified into three categories, high-tech innovations, mid-tech solutions and low-tech/community-based approaches. These two events were selected for their complementary profiles, the HUG Innovations Days for its clinical, hospital-based focus, the Healthcare Week Luxembourg for its broader, European perspective.

These three methods contribute in very different ways in portraying the landscape of innovation. Together, they bring a different angle which enables characterizing the impacts of the healthcare sector.

References

De Lucia, S., Barras, A., & Brulé, G. (2025a). *Frugal innovation in healthcare in a hyper-technological world* [Poster].

De Lucia, S., Furlan, L., Montano, N., Kherad, O., & EFIM Choosing Wisely Working Group. (2025b). Choosing wisely and climate crisis: Reducing low-value care as a strategy to curb healthcare environmental impact. *Internal and Emergency Medicine.* doi:https://doi.org/10.1007/s11739-025-04063-6

Graedel, T. E., Harper, E. M., Nassar, N. T., Nuss, P., & Reck, B. K. (2015). Criticality of metals and metalloids. *Proceedings of the National Academy of Sciences, 112*(14), 4257–4262. https://doi.org/10.1073/pnas.1500415112

Hemmingsen, M. N., Lau, A., Larsen, A., & Ørholt, M. (2023). The role of bibliometric analyses in plastic surgery—Advantages and disadvantages. *Gland Surgery, 12*(7), 87374–87874.
Kumar, R. (2025). Bibliometric analysis: Comprehensive insights into tools, techniques, applications, and solutions for research excellence. *Spectrum of Engineering and Management Sciences, 3*(1), 45–62.

Chapter 3
Impacts of the Healthcare Sector

Abstract The healthcare sector has multiple, cumulative impacts on the environment. Among the multiple impacts (use of resources, air pollution, water pollution ...), the relation to global warming under the form of carbon footprint is the most commonly used. Other methods of impact categorization are secondary in terms of intensity in scientific literature as revealed by the bibliometric analysis. However, there are some blind spots in the carbon footprint literature that other indicators make possible to observe (material intensity, elemental count, water consumption).

Keywords Carbon footprint · Materiality · Impacts · Input · Output · Process

There has always been some form of resource use in the healthcare sector. Excavations in Pompeii have revealed the presence of medical instruments (scalpel, forceps, probes) made of bronze, copper, and iron. In the Middle Ages, sulfur was used for fumigation; mercury was used as a remedy for skin conditions, while copper and lead served as ointments. During the Renaissance, one could find antimony for emetics, vitriol for caustics, and alum for ulcers in the pharmacies. Heat baths used for their therapeutic properties, paricularly for skin conditions, required the continuous burning of wood. As mentioned earlier, the second half of the nineteenth century constituted a pivotal time not only for the increase in longevity but also for the use of resources, with the introduction of X-ray machines (1890s) and the development of electrical surgical and sterilization equipment (1900s). After the Second World War, single-use would be more and more present in healthcare settings. This progression resulted in each step of the care delivery being deeply embedded in material and energy flows. *Diagnostic* procedures rely on imaging technologies that require rare-earth metals for their components (neodymium for the magnets of the MRI or miniature motors of ultrasound, gadolinium as contrast agents, cerium as scintillator material) and consume large quantities of electricity (as a rule of thumb, an MRI scan is equivalent to a 140 km trip with a diesel car). *Acute care and treatment phases* involve energy-intensive equipment (ventilators, surgical robots, robotic arms), HVAC systems (heating, ventilation, and air conditioning), and the omnipresence of single-use plastics, pharmaceuticals, and disposable textiles. *Follow-up care*

G. Brulé, *Reducing the Environmental Impact of Healthcare Systems*, Sustainable Business Development, https://doi.org/10.1007/978-3-032-34889-0_3

and *chronic disease management* frequently depend on transportation of the patients, healthcare workers, family caregivers, the consumption of medicine, and the use of digital monitoring devices.

Main Impacts

The relatively new interest in environmental accounting within the healthcare sector remains quite fragmentary. It is, however, possible to reassemble the *disjecta membra* of different scales and different indicators in order to gain a better understanding of the situation.

At the macro level, the most cited studies (Lancet Countdown, NHS in the United Kingdom, Shift Project in France) show that the healthcare sector contributes to 4–5% of total greenhouse gas emissions (Lenzen et al., 2020; Marrauld et al., 2023; Watts et al., 2018). Taken together, all national healthcare systems emit as if they were the fourth most emitting country in terms of greenhouse gas emissions (less than China, United States, India, but about as much as the whole European Union). However, emissions of greenhouse gases vary significantly across countries, with high-income countries polluting the most in relative terms (and thus, of course in absolute terms) while low- and middle-income countries pollute the least (Karliner et al., 2020). For instance, the HC sector typically represents only 2–3% of national carbon emissions in countries such as India and Indonesia, while in high-income countries such as Switzerland, the United States, or the UK, healthcare systems contribute between 7 and 10% of national emissions.

At the meso level, a large hospital such as HUGs emits around 100,000 t CO_2e, as much as a small city of 10,000–15,000 people. A 40-bed Canadian hospital's footprint at 3500–5000 t CO_2e annually (Cimprich & Young, 2023). As far as emissions in the water are concerned, the particles emitted are so different that they cannot be compared to municipal wastewater (Verlicchi et al., 2012).

At the micro level, it is possible to realize that Swiss healthcare emissions reaching at the individual level represent circa 1 ton CO_2e per capita annually (Mermillod et al., 2024), which represents the target of all activities according to Paris Agreement targets (Nicolet et al., 2022). This means that healthcare per person alone currently represents what all other activities *combined* (food, transport, housing, consumption, etc.) should not exceed. Next, different indicators must be meshed. When taking a systemic lens, one can cite three large families of impacts: input (what goes in), process (what is used to transform/produce), and outputs (what goes out). From an input perspective, one is generally concerned with the amount of resources used to deliver a certain service or to produce a given good as well as the pollution produced in the extraction phase.1 From a healthcare perspective, one can think of the production of plastics, the extraction of helium or the delivery of antibiotics. Process impacts are about the resources used directly onsite, such as the amount of electricity used for MRI or the amount of water consumed in a dialysis process. Output perspectives are about the wastes, emissions, and residues produced by the system (plastics, medicine residues, used materials, greenhouse gas…). First, *input indicators* give us an indication of the resource consumption. In the United States, healthcare consumes over 2000 kg of materials per capita annually (Eckelman et al.,

2020). This includes not only wastes and plastics but also construction materials and pharmaceuticals. A single MRI machine consumes more than 100,000 kWh per year, which represents the equivalent of 20 households' annual electricity use (Roletto et al., 2026). Dialysis procedures consume hundreds of liters of water per session (Connor et al., 2010). Scope 3 emissions (indirect emissions from supply networks) account for 60–80% of healthcare's carbon footprint but remain largely unmeasured due to supply chain opacity (Singleton et al., 2022). Then, *process indicators* give an idea of the operational impacts. Operating rooms, which require 20–40 air changes per hour and energy consumption 3–5 times higher than standard commercial buildings (MacNeill et al., 2024) produce 20–30% of total hospital waste despite occupying only 3–6% of floor space (Thiel et al., 2015). Anesthetic gases, particularly desflurane, have global warming potentials 2500 times that of CO_2, yet usage patterns vary widely without clinical justification (Sherman et al., 2019). Finally, *output indicators* make it possible to see what goes back in the environment. Hospitals in the United States generate over five million tons of waste per year. Single-use have increased by 25% over the last decade, driven by the response to the COVID-19 pandemic, which saw peaks at 200–370% (Klemeš et al., 2020; Peng et al., 2020). This results in feedback loops where health damages are caused by the healthcare system itself. In 2018, loss of 388,000 disability-adjusted life-years (DALYs), deaths and illnesses were attributable to the sector's own pollution in the United States (Eckelman et al., 2020). Comparable results are found in Europe (Richie, 2024). This means mortality caused by healthcare-related pollutions is close to mortality caused by medical errors. Over 60 tons of pharmaceuticals have been detected in Lake Geneva alone and more than one-quarter of 258 rivers worldwide contain drug concentrations at toxic levels (Aus der Beek et al., 2016). Antimicrobial resistance (AMR), driven partly by pharmaceutical environmental contamination, is projected to cause ten million deaths annually by 2050 based on the current scenario (O'Neill, 2016).

Comprehensive methods such as Life Cycle Assessment (LCA) and carbon footprint analysis integrate across all three stages. These different spheres are far from disconnected from each other and just need a common language to communicate. In the same way economists translate social or environmental aspects into economic terms through cost-benefit analysis and environmental valuation, environmentalists mostly translate the use of material or the disposal of materials into greenhouse gas equivalents through methods like carbon footprinting methodologies (Table 3.1).

The predominance of the carbon footprint is not indisputable (Brulé, 2022; Lazarevic & Martin, 2016), but the easiness to understand was part of its success in bringing the complexity of the sustainable ethos in understandable terms. Without going here into an expert debate, the main criticism is the one addressed to any aggregated measure, which is that carbon footprint "flattens" the complexity of the real world by projecting everything on a single axis. *Per hunc processum*, other impacts, such as biodiversity, which are just as important as to the complexity of the living are then overshadowed by climate change. In the case of healthcare, many important parts can be invisibilized by the adoption of carbon footprint (e.g., consumption of water, medical pollution). Furthermore, framing all aspects

Table 3.1 Measures used to document the reduction of environmental impacts of healthcare

Methodological approach	Results
Carbon footprint	73
Life cycle assessment (LCA)	21
Ecological footprint	5
Pharmaceutical pollution	3

Dates All. See Appendix A for more information

into carbon footprint can mislead non-experts and policymakers that all material problems are simply energy and GHG problems, when in reality these domains are deeply intertwined through resource extraction, manufacturing processes, and waste streams. A healthcare system running on perfectly green energy, emitting not a single molecule of greenhouse gas would still release antibiotic-resistant pathogens, endocrine-disrupting pharmaceuticals and microplastics into ecosystems, drinking water, and food chain.

On top of this, these bring ethical issues and geopolitical matters as many resources necessary to create the conditions for energy transition are based in low- or middle-income countries, many in Africa, Asia or Latin America, and extraction often leads to social and environmental problems there. For instance, most of the cobalt, which is a key mineral to energy transition is extracted in RDC (80% of the worldwide production) in very bad conditions for the local workers, often children, and communities to the benefits of some multinationals (Baumann-Pauly, 2020; Williams et al., 2021). On top of this, cobalt is a byproduct of other minerals such as copper and nickel, which means its extraction requires a large amount of ore mining and material extraction. According to the Cobalt institute, to obtain 1 kg of Cobalt, one must extract 30 to 50 kg of minerals. The burden of mortality (through accidents) and diseases (through inhalation and ingestion), also by children is carried by the Global South. Otherwise said, the fantasized immateriality of a fully electric, sustainable system, reified by the prism of the carbon footprint, is in fact deeply material. However, these effects are disregarded by western neocolonialism.

A more prudent way to account for environmental impacts is to combine at least two reading prisms to understand the impacts of the healthcare system on the environment (see also Andrieu et al., 2023 for similar arguments).

> Health-care's resource footprints include non-metallic minerals (used for the construction of buildings, such as hospitals), metal ores (used for the production of buildings and machines), or fossil fuels (used to produce drugs, build hospitals, or power ambulances). (Andrieu et al., p. 747)

> To navigate back inside planetary boundaries, health-care environmental strategies must be broader than greenhouse gases and include objectives in terms of resource use. (ibid., p. 756)

Our choice here is to examine two complementary reading prisms: energy flows and material flows. The first focuses on energy metrics such as carbon footprint and direct energy consumption. The second prism encompasses both the quantity of materials (material use, water consumption, ecological footprint) and their qualitative impacts

Table 3.2 Type of indicators used in studies to assess reduction of environmental impacts of healthcare delivery

Resource/impact	Input results	Process results	Output results
Materials	17	42	118
Energy/carbon	29	36	127
Water	23	3	17
Pharmaceuticals	35	31	42

Dates All. See Appendix A for more information

(ecotoxicity, pharmaceutical pollution, antimicrobial resistance). These two prisms show different angles of the same reality (Table 3.2).

Beyond Carbon

Climate change was called the main systemic threat for humanity by UN Secretary-General António Guterres. But so is the loss of the diversity, the acidification of the ocean or antimicrobial resistance. Completing carbon studies with other views make it possible to look at the repertoire of impacts. The planetary boundaries framework operationalizes strong sustainability by identifying nine Earth system processes that regulate planetary stability (Rockström et al., 2009). Healthcare systems affect all planetary boundaries including climate system stability through greenhouse gas emissions, biodiversity integrity through pharmaceutical pollution and resource extraction, biogeochemical flows through manufacturing and waste disposal, chemical pollution through novel pharmaceutical entities, and freshwater use through water-intensive operations.

Carbon footprint alone cannot suffice to capture the multidimensionality of environmental impacts. In a study comparing 4000 products (Laurent et al., 2012), carbon footprint was often uncorrelated to other environmental impacts such as toxic substance emissions. This means that using carbon footprint only could lead to blind spots or even worse compensation from one impact on another if one was to optimize based on carbon footprint. For instance, burning medical wastes may lead to less production of methane (x 28–34 times more Global Warming Potential over hundred years (GWP100) than CO_2) compared to landfill decomposition and may thus be preferred but could lead to contamination of air or water. Multiple studies stress the fact that comprehensive environmental assessment must reach beyond carbon metrics (Lazarevic & Martin, 2016; Picasso et al., 2014; Solarin, 2020). This is particularly true for the healthcare sector. While healthcare accounts for 4–8% of national carbon footprints globally it also significantly impacts material extraction (13%), blue water consumption (7.5%), land use (7.2%), and waste generation (4.2%) (Steenmeijer et al., 2022) (Fig. 3.1).

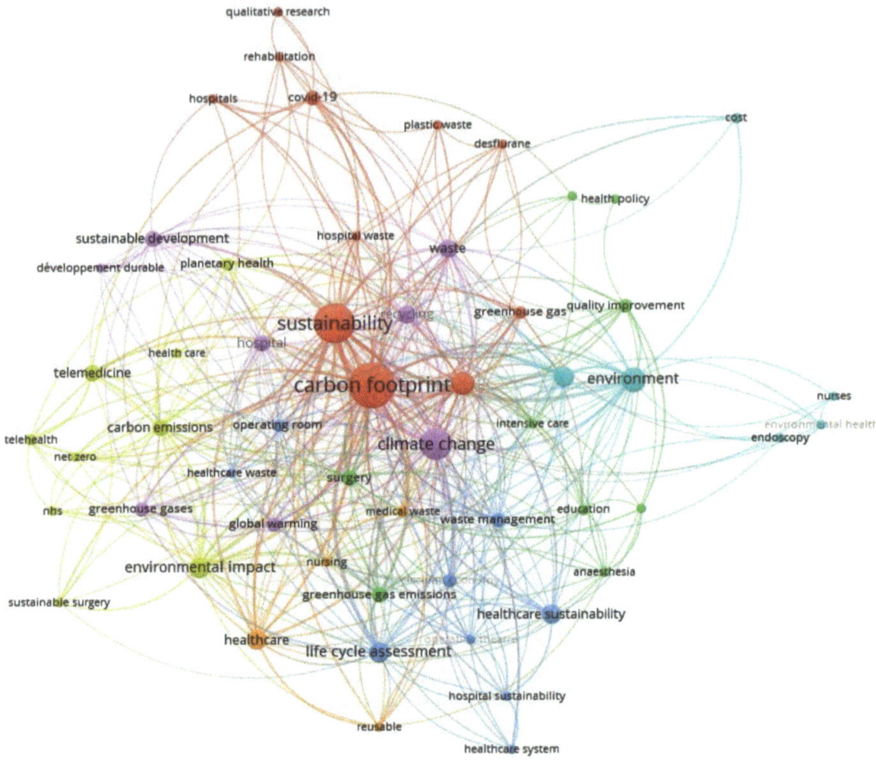

Fig. 3.1 Cloud of words based on the literature on the reduction of healthcare emissions. *Source* Vosviewer analysis based on the bibliography of the book

Beyond Output Indicators

Our analysis of healthcare sustainability literature demonstrates a clear focus on output measures, as compared to input indicators and process indicators. This imbalance is clearer for materials, despite materials constituting the majority of healthcare's physical footprint. Only for water is the input the most important, showing that it is merely considered as a resource to be used. This "end-of-pipe" paradigm mostly addresses symptoms (waste bins, smokestacks) rather than root causes (material intensity, clinical decision-making, supply chain over-complexity). This is particularly questionable as Scope 3 emissions, accounting for 60–80% of healthcare's carbon footprint but generated through procurement and supply chains (INPUT), remain systematically unmeasured (NHS England, 2022).

Environmental Accounting

Energy in the large sense (energy use, carbon footprint, greenhouse gases emissions) is without any doubt the first and the most used entry when discussing environmental impacts of the healthcare system (see Table 3.4). This is true historically as the first study looking at the environmental impact of a national system, the UK NHS was done using carbon footprint (NHS, 2009). The four most cited studies on the impact of the healthcare system all tackle energy or climate issues.[1] On top of the NHS report, which is of the most cited (Pichler et al., 2019) revealed that healthcare systems worldwide were contributing 4–10% of national emissions, a figure that has been used, reused and quoted. Malik et al. (2018) published an article on the carbon footprint of Australian health care in The Lancet, which signaled that environmental concerns were central to health matters. Eckelman & Sherman (2016) zoomed on the US system, the world's largest healthcare system, highlighting that it was generating more emissions than entire countries like the UK. This was replicated by most studies aiming for national or regional accounting of healthcare systems with a comparable methodology like the Shift in France and researchers in Geneva (Marrauld et al., 2023; Mermillod et al., 2024). Most of these studies insist on the Scope 3 emissions, in particular production of pharmaceuticals and medical devices. This was also the methodology used by studies comparing the impact of national healthcare system done by Healthcare Without Harm (Karliner et al., 2020). At the meso level, most studies are also based on the carbon footprint (Alshqaqeeq et al., 2020). When environmental accounting is performed at the unit level, this is largely using a carbon footprint lens (see, e.g., for radiology, Ditac et al., 2023; for pediatrics, Hansen et al., 2023; for oncology, Malmberg et al., 2024; for radiology, Roletto et al., 2024; for endoscopy, Siau et al., 2021). Operating rooms account for disproportionate emissions due to high HVAC needs and large volumes of single-use materials (Sullivan et al., 2023) (Fig. 3.2).

Energy is quite easy to measure, allows for comparison between hospitals and countries. If carbon footprint is already omitting many impacts when used on its golden standard mode, i.e., cradle to grave (extraction of the required materials to disposal of the used products or equipment), this is even more true for many of these studies in which only a part of the scope is studied, for instance cradle to gate (extraction to use in hospital, thus leaving aside the downstream emissions). Some adopt an even narrower focus with only the use of the energy on site considered. Most of these methodological restrictions are understandable. Practitioners are often not trained as environmental specialists, and they seek for actionable measures directed to "hot spots". Plus, data on mining and disposal is often scarce (tons of metal ore or non-metallic minerals). On the output side, these methodologies fail to track what happens after care delivery (residues, emissions, microplastics, antibiotics resistance). Overall, these methodological restrictions tend to restrict the scope of action together with the scope of the study by making problems related to extraction and downfall emissions invisible.

Although less present, the materiality of the healthcare system is far from absent. At the macro level, the amount of waste produced by the different healthcare systems is often studied. The amount of waste produced by national systems has been studied in various contexts (Eker & Bilgili, 2011; Sepetis et al., 2025; Shrank et al., 2019;

[1] The top four articles are cited to date (October 10, 2025) respectively 1118 (Eckleman & Sherman), 854 citations (NHS), 602 (Malik et al), 838 (Pichler et al)

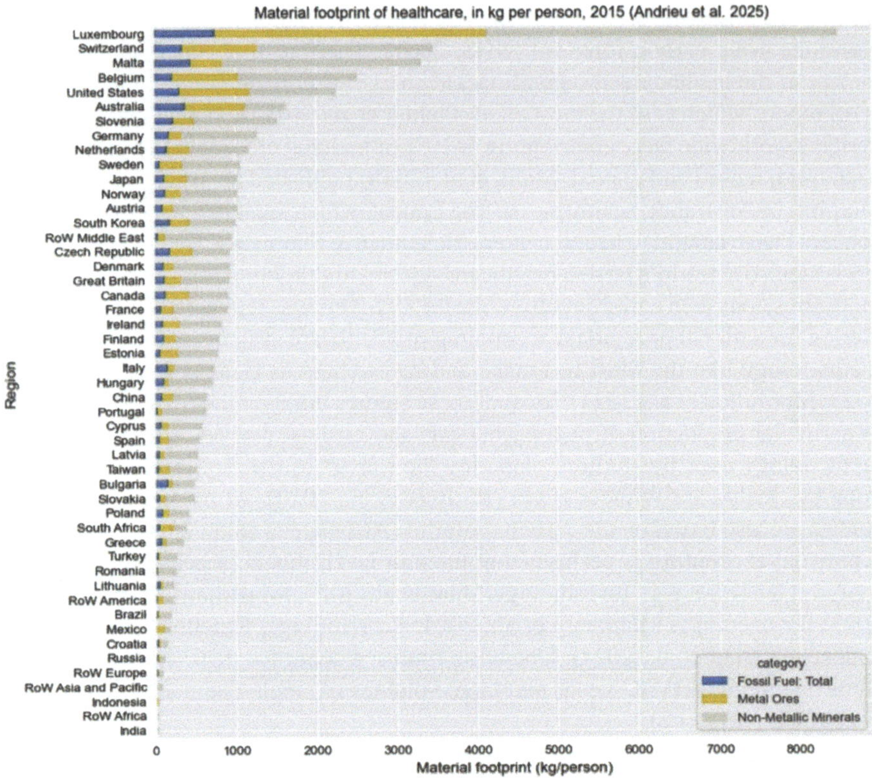

Fig. 3.2 Material footprint of the healthcare sector (Credits: Thomas Gibon) Details in Appendix C

Tudor et al., 2005). One study compared the healthcare system using resource intensity (Andrieu et al., 2023). The literature on materiality in healthcare is relatively scarce and fragmented. Some studies use well-established Life Cycle Assessments (LCAs) of certain devices, drugs or procedures, others quantify the amount of waste per bed, the amount of pharmaceuticals in water, the quantity of plastics, etc.

Waste generation shows impressive numbers. The NHS in England produces over 100,000 tons of clinical waste annually. Hospitals in Peru produce on average 4.89 kg of waste per bed per day (Tudor et al., 2005). Water demand is also very important, as illustrated by the fact that hospitals in Greece consume between 400 and 1200 liters per bed per day. High-income countries demonstrate dramatically higher material footprints in healthcare, with Luxembourg, Switzerland, and Malta exceeding 4000 kg per person annually, versus a few hundred kilograms for LMICs.

Once material flows are examined, it becomes clear how much material is used in healthcare settings. Operating rooms generate vast quantities of disposable gowns, syringes, drapes, and packaging, much of it hazardous and requiring energy-intensive incineration (Eker & Bilgili, 2011). Pharmaceutical residues and contrast agents enter

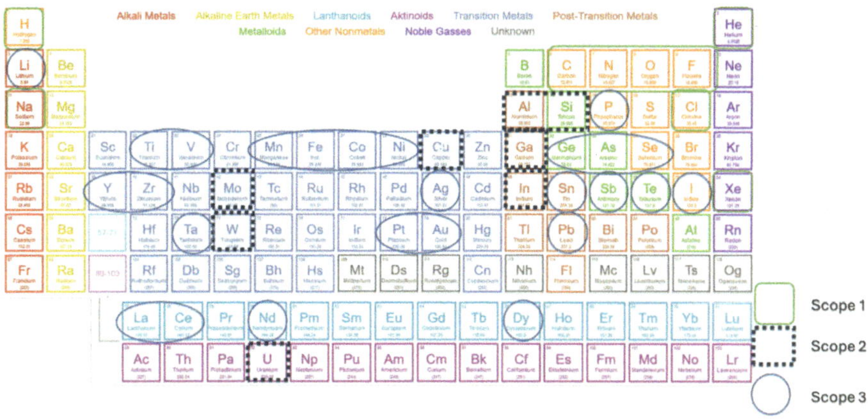

Fig. 3.3 Elements likely used in the healthcare process

wastewater, creating downstream toxicity (Cizmas et al., 2015). Imaging equipment such as MRI and CT scanners incorporate rare earths and specialty metals, which are alsmost never recovered after disposal.

The number of chemical elements (which we call here *elemental count*) is important in many ways. As the number of elements increase, the recyclability decreases. Worse still, the recycling narrative (or downstream tropism) invisibilizes the fact that most equipment is bound to destruction, transfer to low- and middle-income countries and "energetic valorization", which is the world for burning what we said we would recycle (Le Meur, 2021). The more elements we add in a given system, the more we create "hybrid monsters" (Braungart & McDonough, 2009). This raw picture finds an echo when looking at a single healthcare trajectory. In the example below, we highlight the number of materials which are likely to be present in the simplified case of a 62-year old woman coming for a lack of breath and fatigue (Fig. 3.3).

A banal story deeply embedded in materials

After several weeks of unexplained fatigue and lack of breath, a 62-year-old woman is referred for a **high-resolution MRI scan**, which uses superconducting magnets made from **niobium (Nb), very likely produced in Brazil** and cooling with **helium (He)**. The scanner's detectors are made with **gadolinium (Gd)**, a rare earth coming from China, while the servers that process the images rely on **silicon (Si)** semiconductors, **copper (Cu)** wiring, and **gold (Au)** connectors. The screens use LEDs made of nitrogen (N), indium (In) and Gallium (Ga), which are largely produced or refined in China (or South Korea and Japan for indium refining). After radiologists detect a pulmonary lesion, she undergoes surgery assisted by a robot, whose frame is composed of titanium (Ti), **vanadium (V)**, and **chromium (Cr)** alloys. The magnets of its actuators use **neodymium (Nd)** and **dysprosium (Dy)** while the feedback sensors contain **antimony (Sb)** and **tellurium (Te)**. These four elements, two rare earths and two metalloids, depend on Chinese mining and/or refining (especially rare earths and antimony). Other elements are used for the chips of the robot such as **arsenic (As)** and **germanium (Ge), another critical metalloid extracted in China (or possibly Canada or Belgium)**. The **surgical instruments contain iron (Fe), nickel (Ni), manganese (Mn), copper (Cu)** and **zinc (Zn)**. The autoclaves used in the process of sterilization are made of **molybdenum (Mo)** and **tungsten (W). These two transition metals have most of their production in China (or Chile or the United States).** Monitoring devices use electrodes made of **silver (Ag)** and **platinum (Pt)**, the latter being extracted in South African mines. The anesthesia system uses **oxygen (O)**, **nitrogen (N)**, and **xenon (Xe)**. The surgical lights use **yttrium (Y), europium (Eu)**, and **terbium (Tb), a rare earth from China used** to produce high-contrast light. After the operation, the patient receives IV fluids in **plastic bags** stabilized with compounds derived from **chlorine (Cl)** and tubing that may contain **fluorine (F)**. On top of pain medications and antibiotics, which are "basic" organic compounds with **carbon (C), hydrogen (H), nitrogen (N)**, and **oxygen (O)**, routine **blood tests** require reagents whose formulation usually contain **boron (B), sulfur (S), phosphorus (P)** or **iodine (I)**. She's discharged with a **wearable heart monitor** powered by **lithium (Li)** batteries and flexible electronics using **tin (Sn), aluminum (Al)**, and **selenium (Se)**. The app that tracks her recovery connects to cloud-based services on servers powered by chips incorporating **tantalum (Ta)** and **lanthanum (La), a transition metal and a rare earth from respectively Rwanda or DRC and China**. The optical fibers enabling her **teleconsultation** are doped with **erbium (Er), a rare earth from China, the USA or Australia**.

Impacts-Take Away

Key numbers
Based on the Paris agreement, a Swiss person should emit 1 ton per person per year for all of his/her living. That is what is currently (2025) emitted only for his/her health.
Dialysis procedures can consumes hundreds 300-600of liters of water per week, 15′000–30′000 liters/year (https://www.cdc.gov/dialysis-safety/hcp/recommendations-resources/water-use-in-dialysis.html).
A single MRI machine can consume up to 200,000 kWh per year, the equivalent to the annual electricity usage of 20 households; emits as much CO2e as a diesel car riding 140 km per exam.
Hospitals generate over five million tons of waste annually in the US alone.

In 2018, healthcare's greenhouse gas and toxic air pollutant emissions resulted in the loss of 388,000 disability-adjusted life-years in the US (equivalent to the burden of brain cancers (source: GBD 2017).
In 2050, antibiotic resistance will be responsible for the death of 10 millions person per year (about a third of global antibiotics are used for human, the rest for veterinary uses).
At least 60 tons of medicine are present in Lake Geneva.
More than 1/4 of 258 rivers worldwide are polluted with drugs to toxic levels https://www.unep.org/news-and-stories/story/what-fuelling-worlds-antimicrobial-resistance-crisis
In countries such as Luxembourg, Switzerland, and Malta, the material footprint per capita exceeds 4 tons per person annually.

Mapping the System: From Resources to Impacts

We can look at the healthcare sector in a linear way that goes from resources to the healthcare sector and then back to the planet.

Gaïa Resources: this represents the elements our healthcare resources derive from the Earth. These are ecosystems (water, air), resources (mineral, metals, fossil fuels) as well as biological resources that are used.

Gaia-Outcomes encompass what goes out of healthcare into the environment, e.g., emissions of greenhouse gases, pharmaceutical compounds, plastics and microplastics, and electronic waste. These contribute to impacts such as global warming, land use change, air and water pollution, and biodiversity loss.

Technosphere-IN represents the transformation of fossil fuels, metals, minerals, biological resources, and water into plastics, pharmaceuticals, medical devices, electronics, and infrastructure that form the material basis of healthcare delivery.

Technosphere-OUT represents all the extrants leaving the technosphere, whether under solid form (wastes, e-wastes, plastics), liquid form (polluted water), or gaseous form (greenhouse gases, VOCs, other gases).

The *Sociosphere* is an umbrella term that covers the social fabrics in which healthcare is embedded at multiple scales. Macro-level forces include aspects related to economic conditions, demography, policy, supply chain, and culture. Meso-level dynamics encompass organizational cultures, protocols, guidelines, professional norms, social capital, and power dynamics. Micro-level factors involve staff and patient aspirations, environmental literacy, and personal values.

Innovations are initiatives that aim to reduce the environmental impacts as proposed in the graph and in the upcoming chapters. Nine forms of innovation under three main types of innovation: technoproductive innovation, socio-organizational innovation, and paradigmatic innovation (Fig. 3.4).

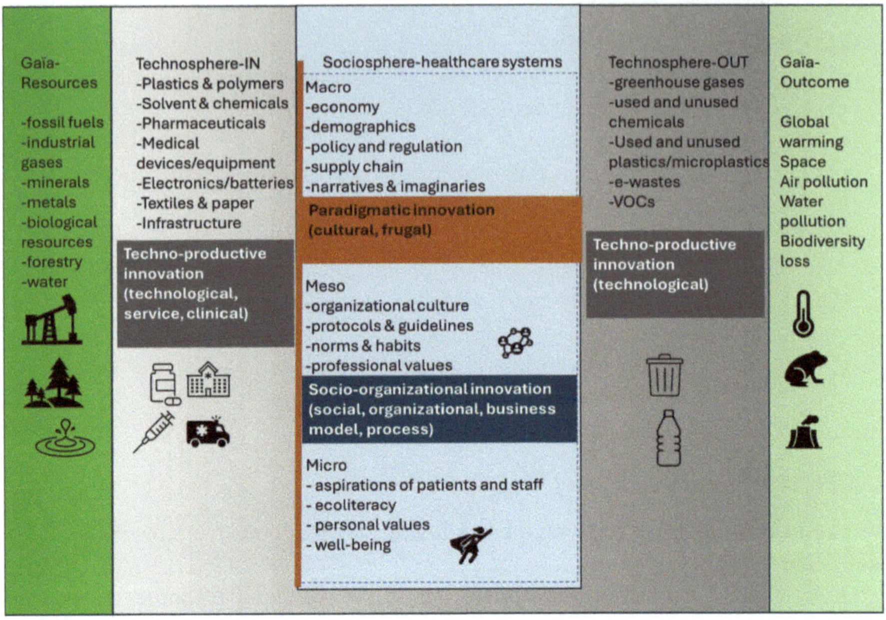

Fig. 3.4 Exchanges between the Earth, the technosphere and the sociosphere

References

Alshqaqeeq, F., Esmaeili, M. A., Overcash, M., & Twomey, J. (2020). Quantifying hospital services by carbon footprint: A systematic literature review of patient care alternatives. *Resources, Conservation and Recycling, 154*, 104560.

Andrieu, B., Marrauld, L., Vidal, O., Egnell, M., Boyer, L., & Fond, G. (2023). Health-care systems' resource footprints and their access and quality in 49 regions between 1995 and 2015: An input–output analysis. *The Lancet Planetary Health, 7*(9), e747–e758. https://doi.org/10.1016/S2542-5196(23)00169-9

Aus der Beek, T., Weber, F.-A., Bergmann, A., Hickmann, S., Ebert, I., Hein, A., & Küster, A. (2016). Pharmaceuticals in the environment—Global occurrences and perspectives. *Environmental Toxicology and Chemistry, 35*(4), 823–835.

Baumann-Pauly, D. (2020). Why cobalt mining in the DRC needs urgent attention. *Council on Foreign Relations, 29.*

Braungart, M., & McDonough, W. (2009). Cradle to cradle. *Random House.*. https://books.google.fr/books?hl=fr&lr=&id=13hfHzBstcEC&oi=fnd&pg=PT2&dq=mcdonough+braungart+cradle&ots=IesWcNAPZx&sig=VMx180k0o9IaSKydEN6rQ1lQzYw

Brulé, G. (2022). Evaluation of existing indexes of sustainable Well-being and propositions for improvement. *Sustainability, 14*(2), 1027. https://doi.org/10.3390/su14021027

Cimprich, A., & Young, S. B. (2023). Environmental footprinting of hospitals: Organizational life cycle assessment of a Canadian hospital. *Journal of Industrial Ecology, 27*(5), 1335–1353. https://doi.org/10.1111/jiec.13425

Cizmas, L., Sharma, V. K., Gray, C. M., & McDonald, T. J. (2015). Pharmaceuticals and personal care products in waters: Occurrence, toxicity, and risk. *Environmental Chemistry Letters, 13*(4), 381–394.

Connor, A., Milne, S., Owen, A., Boyle, G., Mortimer, F., & Stevens, P. (2010). Toward greener dialysis: A CASE study to illustrate and encourage the salvage of reject water. *Journal of Renal Care, 36*(2), 68–72. https://doi.org/10.1111/j.1755-6686.2010.00153.x

Ditac, G., Cottinet, P.-J., Quyen Le, M., Grinberg, D., Duchateau, J., Gardey, K., Dulac, A., Delinière, A., Haddad, C., & Boussuge-Roze, J. (2023). Carbon footprint of atrial fibrillation catheter ablation. *Europace, 25*(2), 331–340.

Eckelman, M. J., Huang, K., Lagasse, R., Senay, E., Dubrow, R., & Sherman, J. D. (2020). Health care pollution and public health damage in the United States: An update: Study examines health care pollution and public health damage in the United States. *Health Affairs, 39*(12), 2071–2079. https://doi.org/10.1377/hlthaff.2020.01247

Eker, H. H., & Bilgili, M. S. (2011). Statistical analysis of waste generation in healthcare services: A case study. *Waste Management & Research: The Journal for a Sustainable Circular Economy, 29*(8), 791–796. https://doi.org/10.1177/0734242X10396755

Hansen, E. E., Chiem, J. L., Righter-Foss, K., Zha, Y., Cockrell, H. C., Greenberg, S. L., Low, D. K., & Martin, L. D. (2023). Project SPRUCE: Saving our planet by reducing carbon emissions, a pediatric anesthesia sustainability quality improvement initiative. *Anesthesia & Analgesia, 137*(1), 98–107.

Karliner, J., Slotterback, S., Boyd, R., Ashby, B., Steele, K., & Wang, J. (2020). Health care's climate footprint: The health sector contribution and opportunities for action. *European Journal of Public Health, 30*(Supplement_5), ckaa165-843.

Klemeš, J. J., Van Fan, Y., & Jiang, P. (2020). The energy and environmental footprints of COVID-19 fighting measures–PPE, disinfection, supply chains. *Energy, 211*, 118701.

Laurent, A., Olsen, S. I., & Hauschild, M. Z. (2012). Limitations of carbon footprint as indicator of environmental sustainability. *Environmental Science & Technology (Washington), 46*(7), 4100–4108. https://doi.org/10.1021/es204163f

Lazarevic, D., & Martin, M. (2016). Life cycle assessments, carbon footprints and carbon visions: Analysing environmental systems analyses of transportation biofuels in Sweden. *Journal of Cleaner Production, 137*, 249–257.

Le Meur, M. (2021). Le mythe du recyclage. *Premier Parallèle.*. https://books.google.fr/books?hl=fr&lr=&id=ciDqEAAAQBAJ&oi=fnd&pg=PA1991&dq=mickaela+lemeur+mythe&ots=3kYVDO9Dxi&sig=wce61xW1iaQ6lOjNWZnzukUGxnM

Lenzen, M., Malik, A., Li, M., Fry, J., Weisz, H., Pichler, P.-P., Chaves, L. S. M., Capon, A., & Pencheon, D. (2020). The environmental footprint of health care: A global assessment. *The Lancet Planetary Health, 4*(7), e271–e279. https://doi.org/10.1016/S2542-5196(20)30121-2

MacNeill, A. J., Rizan, C., & Sherman, J. D. (2024). Improving sustainability and mitigating the environmental impact of anaesthesia and surgery along the perioperative journey: A narrative review. *British Journal of Anaesthesia, 133*(6), 1397–1409. https://doi.org/10.1016/j.bja.2024.05.042

Malmberg, R., Loosveld, J. H., Schilte, H.-P., Burdorf, A., & Van Leeuwen, R. W. (2024). Effect of alternative dosing strategies of pembrolizumab and nivolumab on health-care emissions in The Netherlands: A carbon footprint analysis. *The Lancet Planetary Health, 8*(11), e915–e923.

Marrauld, L., Egnell, M., Verneuil, B., & Rambaud, T. (2023). Soigner les patients tout en soignant la planète: Le bilan carbone du système de santé français et ses leviers de réduction. *Médecine Des Maladies Métaboliques, 17*(4), 318–325.

Mermillod, B., Tornare, R., Jochum, B., Ray, N., & Flahault, A. (2024). Estimating the carbon footprint of healthcare in the Canton of Geneva and reduction scenarios for 2030 and 2040. *International Journal of Environmental Research and Public Health, 21*(6), 690.

NHS. (2009). *NHS England carbon emissions carbon Footprinting report, September 2008 (updated august 2009).* London, UK.

Nicolet, J., Mueller, Y., Paruta, P., Boucher, J., & Senn, N. (2022). What is the carbon footprint of primary care practices? A retrospective life-cycle analysis in Switzerland. *Environmental Health, 21*(1), 3. https://doi.org/10.1186/s12940-021-00814-y

O'Neill, J. (2016). Tackling drug-resistant infections globally: Final report and recommendations. https://www.cabidigitallibrary.org/doi/full/10.5555/20173071720.

Picasso, V. D., Modernel, P. D., Becoña, G., Salvo, L., Gutiérrez, L., & Astigarraga, L. (2014). Sustainability of meat production beyond carbon footprint: A synthesis of case studies from grazing systems in Uruguay. *Meat Science, 98*(3), 346–354. https://doi.org/10.1016/j.meatsci.2014.07.005

Pichler, P.-P., Jaccard, I. S., Weisz, U., & Weisz, H. (2019). International comparison of health care carbon footprints. *Environmental Research Letters, 14*(6), 064004.

Richie, C. (2024). Environmental sustainability and the paradox of prevention. *Journal of Medical Ethics, 50*(8), 534–538.

Rockström, J., Steffen, W., Noone, K., Persson, Å., Chapin, F. S., III, Lambin, E. F., Lenton, T. M., Scheffer, M., Folke, C., & Schellnhuber, H. J. (2009). A safe operating space for humanity. *Nature, 461*(7263), 472–475.

Roletto, A., Zanardo, M., Bonfitto, G. R., Catania, D., Sardanelli, F., & Zanoni, S. (2024). The environmental impact of energy consumption and carbon emissions in radiology departments: A systematic review. *European Radiology Experimental, 8*(1), 35. https://doi.org/10.1186/s41747-024-00424-6

Roletto, A., Verga, M., Savio, A., Viganò, G. L., & Zanoni, S. (2026). Energy performance of MRI systems: On-site validation and comparison with manufacturer declarations. *European Radiology Experimental, 10*(1), 3.

Sepetis, A., Rizos, F., Parlavantzas, I., Zaza, P. N., & Nikolaou, I. E. (2025). Environmental costs in healthcare system: The case studies of Greece health care. *BMC Health Services Research, 25*(1), 522.

Sherman, J. D., MacNeill, A., & Thiel, C. (2019). Reducing pollution from the health care industry. *JAMA, 322*(11), 1043–1044.

Shrank, W. H., Rogstad, T. L., & Parekh, N. (2019). Waste in the US health care system: Estimated costs and potential for savings. *JAMA, 322*(15), 1501–1509.

Singleton, J. A., Lau, E. T., & Nissen, L. M. (2022). An exploration of hospital pharmacists' engagement with sustainability policy in the NHS England. *International Journal of Pharmacy Practice, 30*(4), 383–390.

Siau, K., Hayee, B., & Gayam, S. (2021). Endoscopy's current carbon footprint. *Techniques and Innovations in Gastrointestinal Endoscopy, 23*(4), 344–352.

Solarin, S. A. (2020). An environmental impact assessment of fossil fuel subsidies in emerging and developing economies. *Environmental Impact Assessment Review, 85*, 106443. https://doi.org/10.1016/j.eiar.2020.106443

Steenmeijer, M. A., Rodrigues, J. F. D., Zijp, M. C., & Waaijers-van Der Loop, S. L. (2022). The environmental impact of the Dutch health-care sector beyond climate change: An input–output analysis. *The Lancet Planetary Health, 6*(12), e949–e957. https://doi.org/10.1016/S2542-5196(22)00244-3

Thiel, C. L., Eckelman, M., Guido, R., Huddleston, M., Landis, A. E., Sherman, J., Shrake, S. O., Copley-Woods, N., & Bilec, M. M. (2015). Environmental impacts of surgical procedures: Life cycle assessment of hysterectomy in the United States. *Environmental Science & Technology, 49*(3), 1779–1786. https://doi.org/10.1021/es504719g

Tudor, T. L., Noonan, C. L., & Jenkin, L. E. T. (2005). Healthcare waste management: A case study from the National Health Service in Cornwall. *United Kingdom. Waste Management, 25*(6), 606–615.

Verlicchi, P., Al Aukidy, M., Galletti, A., Petrovic, M., & Barceló, D. (2012). Hospital effluent: Investigation of the concentrations and distribution of pharmaceuticals and environmental risk assessment. *Science of the Total Environment, 430*, 109–118.

Watts, N., Amann, M., Ayeb-Karlsson, S., Belesova, K., Bouley, T., Boykoff, M., ... & Costello, A. (2018). The Lancet Countdown on health and climate change: From 25 years of inaction to a global transformation for public health. *The Lancet, 391*(10120), 581–630.

Williams, J. T., Vangu, A. M., Mabiala, H. B., Mangungulu, H. B., & Tissingh, E. K. (2021). Toxicity in the supply chain: Cobalt, orthopaedics, and The Democratic Republic of the Congo. *The Lancet Planetary Health, 5*(6), e327–e328.

Chapter 4
Innovation(S)

Abstract Innovation is not unidimensional, neither in absolute terms nor in the specific field of reducing the environmental impacts of the healthcare system. In this chapter, nine forms of innovation are presented in the three families of innovation (technoproductive, socio-organizational, paradigmatic). Each form of innovation is presented with its pros and cons regarding its potential for sustainability.

Keywords Innovation · Invention · Oslo manual · Sustainability · Impacts

In the middle of the nineteenth century, the River Thames had become so polluted with sewage that the smells had reached the Parliament and cholera epidemics had started devastating London, resulting in thousands of deaths during different outbreaks (1832, 1849, 1854 and 1866). In *Little Dorit*, Charles Dickens writes: "Miles of close wells and pits of houses, where the inhabitants gasped for air, stretched far away towards every point of the compass. Through the heart of the town a deadly sewer ebbed and flowed, in the place of a fine fresh river". A political debate emerged around the actions to be taken. Edwin Chadwick, a famous figure of modern epidemiology imagined a system integrating the reuse of human excreta and agricultural nutrient cycles, minimizing waste and closing ecological loops. In line with his thoughts, the journalist Henry Mayhew worked on a combination of closed circuits, where waste is transformed back into useful products (e.g., sewage to fertilizer, rags to paper) and open circuits, where excrements and unusable products were discarded, emphasizing an *upstream* vision recognizing how social practices could generate new and unexpected uses that would inevitably generate waste (Leckie, 2020). On the other side of the spectrum, Joseph Bazalgette, a civil engineer, imagined a system based on massive sewer infrastructures. This *downstream* vision was chosen by the parliament, maintaining the *how* (do we get rid of the wastes) and forgetting the *why* (are the wastes produced in the first place). The solution developed by Bazalgette was an undisputable success according to certain metrics such as mortality rates due to cholera or typhoid, less so if considering environmental indicators such as long-term resource use. This was a solution that emerged about two centuries ago. The *environmental cost to solve a health issue* was proportionally less expensive and problematic

G. Brulé, *Reducing the Environmental Impact of Healthcare Systems*, Sustainable Business Development, https://doi.org/10.1007/978-3-032-34889-0_4

in a world of 1 billion individuals than in a world of 8 billion persons. Many environmental transformations or resource use can be justified through health preservation, but since we know "environment" and "health" are much less compartmented than we used to think, the question is what environmental cost for what health gains? This question should not only be adressed at a given time, but examined across decades and generations. This raises many questions that combine health, resource use, environmental justice. We could also add the question of which subpopulations benefit from the progress/are affected by it, but as defined in the scope of the book in the introductory chapter, we leave here geopolitical questions aside as this would require a book on its own and the study of environmental impacts of the healthcare system is already more than a 9–5 job. However, we can illustrate the tension with a hypothetical case: if we were to save 0.1% of the world population, by using 10% of the world resources which will make a horrible life for the equivalent of 50% the population in the coming generations, should we do it? This question is rhetorical and requires less an answer than a reflection, which is how much we gain in terms of health, how much we lose in terms of environment, since we now know that degrading the environment will backfire on health. Also, after having written extensively on indicators, we now believe that they are necessary but not sufficient, since there is always a new environmental problem emerging which wasn't been thought of when the dashboard of indicators was constituted and which becomes a blind spot. In that sense, we need not only indicators but also ethical principles, which act as safeguards of our best practices. In the same way medicine can be guided by Hippocratic principles and evidence-based medicine, sustainability indicators (carbon footprint, resource consumption) are necessary as they measure what we can quantify, but they need to be complemented by principles like precaution, sufficiency, or justice, in order not to be blindsided. There are also many papers trying to propose concrete solutions to reduce the environmental impact of a hospital, a unit or a specific phase of the care process. These are forms of *innovations*. Before examining innovations reducing the environmental impacts of the healthcare sector, let us define the contours of this term as we use it.

What Is Innovation (and What It Is Not)

Innovation plays a central role in our modern societies. Innovation is celebrated at all levels. At the national level, Switzerland was designated for the 15th time most "innovative" country in the world.[1] At the meso level, companies such as Apple or Telsa are usually considered as "innovative". At the individual level, individuals such as Steve Jobs are viewed as "innovators". These labeling occur at very different scales and in very different contexts so let us see if we can find a common denominator.

[1] For critiques on the way this is measured, read here https://www.publiceye.ch/en/topics/pharmaceutical-industry/price-of-medicines-walls-of-abusive-patents-are-standing-in-the-way-of-competition.

In the Oslo manual, which is the reference for the field, innovation is defined as "a new or improved product or process (or combination thereof) that differs significantly from the unit's previous products or processes and that has been made available to potential users (product) or brought into use by the unit (process)". Novelty is therefore always at the core of innovation, although arguably defining significantly what different is difficult (Alter, 2010). Behind that generic and institutional definition, this means innovation is still a very heterogeneous field. In order to better define its contours, we can also define what innovation is not. By going beyond common misconceptions, we can see clearer what innovation can serve in our context.

Innovation is not an invention. Invention is the creation of a product or a process but outside the socio-organizational sphere, whereas innovation is necessarily bound to the social realm. In other words, an invention can occur *in abstracto*, away from the society, whereas an innovation is by definition an invention which has been adopted to some degree. A healthcare worker creating a zero-carbon catheter alone in his laboratory but without external use would be an inventor but not an innovator.

Innovation is not only about products. This appeared clearly since the previous version of the Oslo Manual. In the 2005 version, one can find four subtypes of innovation (product, process, organizational, and marketing). Although this difference was apparently reduced to two main types in the 2018 version (product innovation and business process innovation), each type was subdivided into subcategories. Product innovation is about goods and services, whereas business process innovation includes 6 subcategories (production of goods or services, distribution and logistics, marketing and sales, information and communication systems, administration and management, product and business process development). Innovation thus far exceeds the borders of product innovation.

Innovation does not necessarily occur in private company settings. The later version of the Oslo Manual left a nice part to public innovation and open innovation. This means "value" is not only about number of patents but can also be about improving social problems or reducing environmental impacts. Although innovation has long been restricted to industrial settings and to commercial uses, innovation has then gradually expanded beyond technology, beyond manufacturing and beyond market uses which public and social innovations getting more attention (Gault et al., 2023).

Innovation is far from absolute. It is observer-dependent(van der Kooij, 2017): what appears as radical innovation from a manufacturer's perspective may be incremental from a healthcare worker's perspective. As we shall see later, this framing has consequences because some innovate while mentioning it and others don't.

Innovation is not only an outcome. The literature on innovation is often divided around the question of whether innovation is a product or a process. In the bibliometric analyses we are conducting in the frame of this book, we are, by counting publications, essentially treating innovation as a product. But innovation can also be considered as a messy and iterative process (Van de Ven et al., 1999).

Innovation is not always positive.[2] In an era that can be defined as the *innovatization* of the world (Jeannerat & Crevoisier, 2022), innovation is a term that is positively connoted. However, any critical stance must resist the temptation to uniformly follow the flow and adopt it unquestionably. Long regarded as negative in premodern societies where change was associated as going against divine order (Godin 2012, p. 37), societies have shifted to the opposite, now being prone to a pro-innovation bias (Martuccelli, 2016; Rogers et al., 2014). The Schumpeterian concept of innovation as a *creative destruction* paves the way to understanding that if innovation can bring some positivity (creation) it can also bring negativity (destruction). Arguably, many recent innovations have had a net negative effect (Aggeri, 2023). In recent years, the amount of scholars not only blindly advocating innovation and looking at the negative sides have increased. Scholars have looked into the "dark side of innovation"(Chopra, 2013), the noxious effects of innovation (Biggi & Giuliani, 2022) the "revenge effects" of innovation (Tanner, 1996), the dark side of public innovations (Meijer & Thaens, 2021). Problems can occur at the society level with unemployment, mass displacement of workers or lack of meaning due to permanent changes (Portes, 2021; Sveiby, 2017). There can be issues at the organizational level when seeking innovation such as information loss, incompatibility with culture, exclusion of employees, struggle (Dziurski & Wachowiak, 2021; Mariano & Casey, 2015). Finally, and most relevant to the present book, many innovations, including those framed as "eco-innovations" end up having a negative impact on the environment through rebound effects or Jevon paradox, which although distinct concepts, both highlight the fact that the benefits of eco-innovations decrease with wider use and end up having net negative consequences when aggregated (Ertelt & Carlborg, 2024; Raghutla & Chittedi, 2023). Because it is related to a conception of what is "good", it is deeply normative. Thus, we can't treat innovation as an unquestioned good, but rather as a field of contested values and strategic choices.

Innovation in the Healthcare Sector: What the Literature Reveals

As stated in the introductory chapter of this book, one way to look at the forms of innovation in the healthcare sector is to look at the scientific literature. It depicts at the same time the values and the priorities of a certain field, what is covered and what is not. Let us now act like the geographers of the land of innovation, observe the densest part and the least dense, the points of interest and the deserts. Indirectly, this will bring us information of where the rivers of funding go, where are the areas that are invested and where are the fields of non-interest.

[2] Notable counter-examples about the "dark side of innovation"(Chopra, 2013), the noxious effects of innovation (Biggi & Giuliani, 2022) the "revenge effects"(Tanner, 1996), the dark side of public innovations (Meijer & Thaens, 2021).

Different Divisions of Innovation Beyond Oslo Manual

We have seen that the definitions and the forms of innovation are diverse. Innovation-as-an-end or innovation-as-a-process is a structuring division of innovation studies. Radical innovation or incremental innovation is also often used in distinguishing the degree of novelty of new products or processes. Zooming a bit more of what constitutes innovation, high-tech innovation versus low-tech innovation is typically seen as the degree of sophistication of the technology used to reach what is considered as an innovation. When turning toward material or energy, one can distinguish high-resource from low-resource innovations or low-entropy from high-entropy innovations (Georgescu-Roegen, 2013).

Beyond the Oslo Manual, scholars have proposed categorizations that capture innovation's multidimensional nature. In a previous work of ours, we have developed three complementary types of innovation (Jeannerat et al., 2023). *Technoproductive innovations* encompass the development of new products, technologies, and devices. *Social innovations* involve new forms of organization, from service delivery to grassroots movements that restructure the way value is created. Finally, *cultural innovations* transform imaginaries and values. Innovation has also been differentiated as products, processes, positions or paradigms (Tidd & Bessant, 2014). Product innovation refers to the introduction of new or improved goods. Process innovation means transforming the way activities are performed. Position innovation (which is close to what we call here *service innovation*) focuses on changing the way care delivery is provided, e.g., shifting patients with chronic disease from hospitals to community-based settings. Finally, paradigm innovation challenges the underlying narratives. These different categorizations highlight the fact that "innovations are complex and multi-dimensional" and that classification systems should be "more sensitive to innovation multidimensionality" to effectively guide healthcare transformation (Adams et al., 2011).

Apart from a few exceptions, classifications of innovations in the healthcare sector remain limited and fragmented and are unfit for sustainability analysis. As for the general innovation (not specific in the healthcare sector), some distinguish technological from non-technological innovations (Gerush et al., 2024), others degrees of maturity and disruptiveness (Adams et al., 2006), domains of the healthcare sector (basic science, education, processes, technique, see (Sounderajah et al., 2021)). Finally, some others focus on one or several subtypes of innovation but lack a theoretical framework to explicit environmental matters. For instance, Mishra and Jain (2025) build upon Herzlinger (2006) to develop several forms of innovation and present a framework which is finer than most of the existing ones in the literature. Yet, the granularity is too coarse for sustainability matters as it mixes the various forms of organizational innovation, clinical and technological, organizational/process/social and it lacks a larger paradigmatic view. In other words, to date, there are no comprehensive frameworks that enable to look into the different forms of innovation in the healthcare sector in a way that is actionable for healthcare professionals and

Table 4.1 Indicators and environment (see Appendix D for more details)

	No environmental dimension	Partial environmental	Explicit environmental metrics
Input metrics	3	0	6
Process metrics	4	1	1
Output metrics	7	1	5
Outcome metrics	5	1	5
Total	**19**	**3**	**17**

institutions seeking a grammar of existing innovations to reduce their environmental impacts (Table 4.1).

A Framework of 9 Innovations in the Healthcare Sector for Sustainable Use

On top of these lines of division, one can distinguish different types of innovations. In a previous work of ours, we have developed three complementary types of innovation (Jeannerat et al., 2023). Technoproductive innovations encompass the development of new products, technologies, and devices. Social innovations involve new forms of organization, from service delivery to grassroots movements that restructure the way value is created. Finally, cultural innovations transform imaginaries and values. We here build upon this strand of research to distinguish nine distinct forms of healthcare innovation, organized across three interconnected domains, that collectively address the multifaceted challenges of modern medical systems. **Technoproductive innovations** encompass *technological innovation* (advanced devices, equipment), *clinical innovation* (new treatment methods and medical practices that enhance patient outcomes), *service innovation* (new models of care delivery), and *business model innovation* (new ways of financing and organizing healthcare economics) (Adams et al., 2011; Boyle et al., 2022). **Socio-organizational innovations** include *organizational innovation*, defined by Omachonu and Einspruch (2010) as "the implementation of a new organizational method in the firm's business practices, workplace organization or external relations", *social innovation* (communities and patients' engagement), and *process innovation* (new ways of organizing and delivering care through improved operational workflows). **Paradigmatic innovations** comprise at the same time *cultural innovation* (new collective values, norms, and narratives), for instance questioning cure-centric paradigms (Pozzo et al., 2020) and *frugal innovation*, which provides resource-efficient solutions, achieving *more with less* (Bhatti & Ventresca, 2013).

Brought together, these forms of innovations provide a framework of innovations with a granularity which is fine enough so that healthcare workers and institutions can seek for themselves what best serves their purpose. Each type of innovation is connected to the literature and adapted to the healthcare context. At the highest level, the tripartite structure (technoproductive, socio-organizational, and paradigmatic innovation) draws directly from previous work (Jeannerat, Crevoisier, Brulé and Suter, see below). Building on this conceptual basis, the nine forms of innovation integrate insights from various fields: product, process, organizational, and business model innovation as defined in the Oslo Manual; clinical and service innovation as developed in health research; social and organizational innovation from organizational sociology; and frugal innovation from global health and sustainability research. The present classification is therefore a systematic synthesis aimed at capturing the grammar of innovations that can influence the environmental footprint of healthcare systems.

Figure 4.2 illustrates this integrative framework. The domain of production addresses how materials and infrastructures are developed, manufactured, and deployed. The domain of organization and regulation encompasses protocols, guidelines, organizational cultures, professional praxis and procurement norms that shape what technologies and practices are promoted or resisted. The domain of meaning shapes the imaginaries and values that define what counts as "good care", "modern medicine", or "professional excellence". Environmental sustainability in healthcare is at the center of these three intersecting forms of innovation.

Each domain represents a distinct field of innovation, yet deep transformation requires coordinated action across all three. The following examines innovations within each domain, beginning with the technoproductive innovations that currently dominate healthcare sustainability discourse, then exploring the socio-organizational innovations that could restructure care delivery, and finally investigating the cultural innovations necessary to transform healthcare's underlying cultures and imaginaries.

Technoproductive Innovations

Technoproductive instruments have been long served as responses to environmental challenges. When the Roman Empire was facing urban pollution and waterborne diseases, a network of aquaeducti and a sewage system like the Cloaca Maxima were designed. As the Dutch were facing flooded land and degraded coastal areas from rising seas, they engineered windmill-powered pumping systems combined with a line of dikes. The soil loss due to deforestation in the Andes or Southeast Asia led to the development of terracing technologies such as advanced techniques of draining, geotextiles, and microclimate management. Some first endeavors to reduce the environmental impacts of the healthcare system can be observed some centuries ago, rarely for the environment but for health or practicality matters. As plague was hitting medieval cities, wastes were separated between contaminated and not contaminated, following strict protocols for managing infectious patients and their wastes, and doctors designed leather coats and beaked masks that could serve through multiple outbreaks. Florence Nightingale, although not tackling wastes for the sake of the environment, had erected principles of efficiency that would not be connected to environmental matters until much later (Shaner-McRae & Jas, 2007).

Nowadays, technoproductive innovation has become a dominant answer within the portfolio of answers to reduce the environmental impacts in the different stages of healthcare trajectories (diagnosis, treatment, monitoring). Whether it is in the form of modified equipment, advanced materials, precision medicine, or AI, technoproductive innovation shows promising ways to tackle the environmental impacts of the healthcare system. The underlying diversity of technoproductive answers shows that technology should be understood in the large sense. It does not have to be, say, a robot or medical arm but can also be a protocol, a process, or a business model. Several types of innovation fit under the same banner of technoproductive tools. (Fig. 4.1)

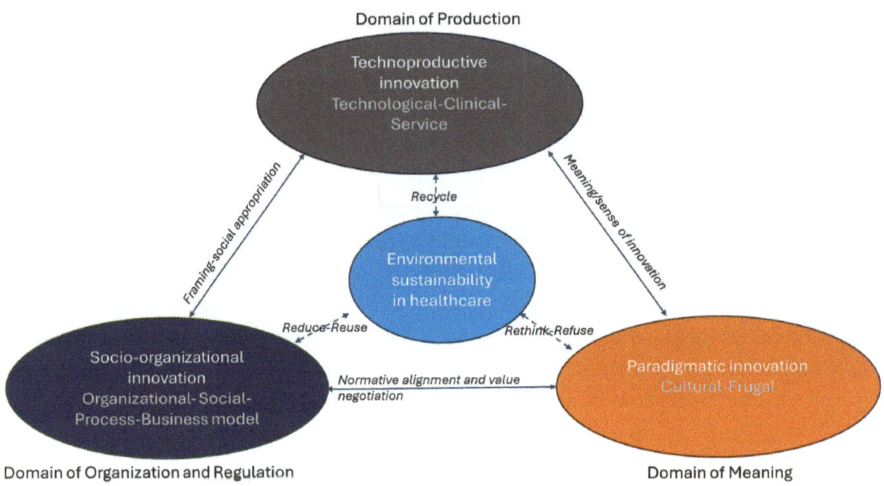

Fig. 4.1 The different forms of innovation for environmental sustainability in healthcare (inspired by Jeannerat et al., 2023)

Technological Innovation

Technological innovation is a rather large subcategory that shows important heterogeneity within the healthcare sector (medicines, medical equipment, hard-tech (AI, machine learning, robots)). It is impossible to fully account for the wide range of technologies that enable reducing environmental impacts as this includes all existing types of innovation as well as all the current aspirations of future health. Pharmaceutical innovations address impacts through upstream green chemistry approaches using water-based solvents and continuous processing (Kar et al., 2022), and downstream advanced wastewater treatment systems using oxidation and membrane filtration (Giakoumakis et al., 2021). Laboratory environmental impacts can be reduced through process innovations (microfluidic technologies reducing reagent volumes) (Devis et al., 2025; Lowden & Henderson, 2025; Tjokro et al., 2025) and downstream solutions (recycling, reactants or adsorbents such as active carbon or zeolites for solvents or pollutants).

The selection of equipment can be a sensible way to reduce environmental impacts of the healthcare sector. A Spanish study shows that shifting 50% of the national prescription from pressurized metered-dose inhalers to dry powder inhalers could prevent 200,000 tons of CO_2 emissions annually (Garin et al., 2025). Choosing echocardiography over cardiac MRI or SPECT scanning reduces carbon emissions by 80–99% (Barratt et al., 2023). Power management systems for MRI machines can save 35–47 MWh annually per machine, reducing electricity costs by $8,050–10,800 (Komenan, 2025). As for contrast agents, upstream solutions (minimization of doses via AI-based dosimetry, use of isotopes with shorter half-lives, multi-CT to optimize or reduce ICM waste), process solutions (collection of patient urine for 24 h, separation of iodinated contrast media and contaminated waste, education of patient on disposal) and downstream solutions (recycling of patient urine via reverse osmosis, storing with wastewater treatment plants, use of peracetic acid for disinfection) can be considered (Leswick et al., 2025). As far as robots are concerned, there are limited evidence of their environmental impacts. One systematic review show that robots-driven procedures generating 43.5% higher emissions than laparoscopic alternatives(6 to 814 kg CO2e per case) (Papadopoulou et al., 2022).

AI and machine-learning technologies may also optimize healthcare operations through data-driven automation (Upadhyay et al., 2023). The environmental impacts of AI for healthcare context is a rather novel topic (Champendal et al., 2025). In one real-world study, autonomous AI, where the machine performs a decision without human approval, could achieve an 80% reduction in greenhouse gas emissions compared to in-person specialist encounters with equivalent clinical outcomes (Wolf et al., 2022). Additional studies suggest AI can reduce emissions through process optimization and resource waste reduction (Bloomfield et al., 2021; Das & Chandra, 2023). However, the infrastructure upon which AI is built also create environmental concerns such as increased energy consumption and electronic waste (Champendal et al., 2025; Mikhailova & Sharova, 2023; Samuel & Lucassen, 2023). The net environmental benefit depends on whether AI's efficiency gains outweigh its own carbon footprint, a calculation that lacks standardized measurement approaches across the healthcare sector (Bloomfield et al., 2021). Most studies have theoretical arguments rather than empirical ones and research shows that only 12% of studies evaluate the full lifecycle environmental impacts of digital technologies (Berger et al., 2025).

Although we focus here on existing innovations, it is important to realize that the most promethean forms of future innovation belong to this category, from genetic engineering pre-birth to ultrapredictive diagnosis, from own-organ-cultivation avoiding any allo-transplantation to transhumanism. As this is upcoming, studies about the environmental impacts are yet absent, but one can imagine that, as for other forms of technological innovation, the benefits (reduction of dialysis, the reduction of illnesses) can also come with environmental costs (extreme competition for rare earth, minerals) and social inequalities in health. Implementation barriers include high upfront capital costs, rapid obsolescence creating vendor lock-in and proprietary systems restricting repair and circular economy (see Appendix E for more details on the barriers).

Anesthetic Gas Capture
A 1,500-bed academic medical center in North America has implemented a technology that traps anesthetic emissions. This system captures waste gases directly from the operating room through the ventilation system and destroys them through catalytic conversion. Combined with switching from desflurane to sevoflurane, the hospital reduced its anesthesia-related greenhouse gas emissions by 95%. The investment paid for itself within 18 months through reduced gas purchasing costs.

Technological innovation at a glance	
Definition	New devices, equipment, materials, and digital tools that introduce novel technical capabilities into healthcare delivery
Key characteristics	Hardware and software-based solutions Capital-intensive and R&D-driven Requires technical infrastructure and specialized expertise
Contexts	Hospitals, clinical facilities, diagnostic laboratories, biomedical engineering departments
Sustainability strengths	Reduction of energy use through energy-efficient devices Reduction of treatment waste through precision medicinc
Sustainability limitations	Electronic waste and recycling difficulties High embodied carbon in manufacturing Dependency on extraction of rare earth minerals and metals
Barriers to implementation	High upfront capital costs Rapid obsolescence creating vendor lock-in Proprietary systems restricting repair and circular economy
Relationship to other innovation types	Service Innovation (e.g., telemedicine platforms) Clinical Innovation (e.g., diagnostic technologies) Process Innovation (e.g., workflow automation tools)
Key indicators	Energy consumption (kWh per procedure/device) Embodied carbon (kg CO_2e in manufacturing) Material circularity (% recyclable/reusable components)
Examples	LED surgical lighting (70% energy reduction) Reprocessed single-use medical devices AI-powered diagnostic algorithms

(continued)

(continued)

Technological innovation at a glance	
Key references	Schumpeter (1942); Freeman & Soete (1997)

Clinical Innovation

As for other forms of innovation, clinical innovation has several definitions. Thus, it includes a series of interventions that are not formally evaluated according to the standards of evidence-based medicine. It is usually described as a non-coded form of innovation in the interstices of evidence-based medicine, which on the contrary represents an encoded form of innovation (Ghaemi & Goodwin, 2007; Wiersma et al., 2025). While definitions vary slightly, they usually rely on deviation from standard practice and potential for improving healthcare delivery. In many examples, clinical innovation is not about developing new products (as in the case of technological innovation, for instance) as to finding new contexts of application for existing products. There are many examples in the psychopharmacology field for instance. In the 1950s, after clinicians observed iproniazid, originally used for tuberculosis, had mood-elevating properties, monoamine oxidase inhibitors (MOAIs) became used for depression. Likewise, a clinician observed that phenothiazines, originally used as anesthetics, had tranquilizing effects, which led to their use for psychosis treatment. Other examples include the use of tricyclic antidepressants, originally developed for schizophrenia and later used for depressive symptoms or carbamazepine, originally used for epileptic patients to patients with bipolar disorders or azidothymidine (AZT), used initially for treating thrombocytopenia of AIDS patients, which ended up increasing life expectancy, due to its antiviral properties. Some of these innovations have environmental benefits, such as minimally invasive procedures (laparoscopic versus open surgery reducing postoperative complications and length of stay), precision diagnostics (selective, indication-based preoperative testing and imaging rather than routine protocols), and personalized medicine approaches including effective type 2 diabetes management that prevents disease progression and associated cardiovascular complications, thereby reducing healthcare resource consumption and carbon emissions by 9–20% per patient while simultaneously providing co-benefits of cost savings, reduced patient time burden, and improved clinical outcomes (Barratt et al., 2023). Genomic therapy shows some promises to move toward a personal, predictive, and preventive medicine, but the costs/benefits in terms of environment is not yet known in the literature although arguably questionable (Jimenez-Sanchez, 2015). As far as minimal invasive procedures are concerned, their impacts are higher as conventional. A study showed that minimally invasive axillary osmidrosis surgery does consume more carbon than conventional techniques (50.48 $kgCO_2e$ vs 38.2 $kgCO_2e$) (Tan & Zhang, 2025) showing that this type of clinical innovation is not so efficient in terms of resource use.

Also, precision medicine has substantial impacts on the environment (Samuel & Lucassen, 2023) with potential for improvement (Sittig et al., 2022). Reversely, some innovations show clear environmental benefit, in particular in the field of anesthesia. Innovations in anesthesia have been numerous in recent years, which is significant for a part of the healthcare delivery which is responsible for about 5% on its own. Switching from desflurane to sevoflurane reduces carbon footprint 40-fold, while gas capture technologies can trap 100% of anesthetic emissions (Gonzalez-Pizarro et al., 2023; Potera, 2012). Targeted drug therapies, including prefilled medication syringes and precision delivery systems can minimize the release of active pharmaceutical ingredients (APIs) into the environment. This approach aligns with "eco-directed sustainable prescribing" strategies (precise, lower-dose prescribing and optimized administration) (Daughton & Ruhoy, 2011). By ensuring that only the required dose reaches the physiological target, this is a form of co-benefit where patient safety, cost efficiency and environmental benefits(resource use, wastes, downstream emissions) collide (Moermond et al., 2022). Implementation barriers include economic incentives (as high-tech procedures are billed much more than low-tech medicine) intertwined with a cultural paradigm of more is better, guidelines that favor resource-intensive practices and a tropism to prefer intervention to watchful waiting (see Appendix E for more details on the barriers).

Precision Diagnostics in Cardiac Care: Echocardiography First

A 1,440-bed in North America has implemented a clinical protocol that prioritizes echocardiography over cardiac MRI or SPECT scanning for initial cardiac assessment on one of its sites. This evidence-based approach reduced carbon emissions by 80–99% per diagnostic procedure while maintaining diagnostic accuracy. This change of equipment for approximately 15,000 annual cardiac imaging studies prevented 450 metric tons of CO_2 emissions yearly and saved $3 million annually. The success led to protocol adoption across the network of a dozen hospitals.

Clinical innovation at a glance	
Definition	New diagnostic, therapeutic, and treatment approaches that change clinical practice and patient care pathways
Key characteristics	Evidence-based medical advancements Requires clinical validation and regulatory approval Driven by medical research and practice evolution
Contexts	Hospitals, clinics, research centers, primary care settings, specialized treatment facilities
Sustainability strengths	Reduction of resource use through targeted therapies Reduction of hospital stays through improved treatments Reduction of adverse events minimizing additional interventions

(continued)

(continued)

Clinical innovation at a glance	
Sustainability limitations	Pharmaceutical production environmental footprint Increased use of single-use sterile equipment Complex drug supply chains and cold chain requirements
Barriers to implementation	Cultural paradigm ("more is better") Guidelines favor resource-intensive practices Intervention preferred to watchful waiting
Relationship to other innovation types	Technological Innovation (e.g., new diagnostic devices enable clinical changes) Process Innovation (e.g., clinical pathways redesign) Service Innovation (e.g., ambulatory care models)
Key indicators	Avoided procedures (% reduction in unnecessary interventions) Length of stay reduction (days saved per patient) Pharmaceutical waste (kg medications avoided/reduced)
Examples	Minimally invasive surgical techniques reducing recovery times Point-of-care diagnostics eliminating laboratory transport Personalized oncology reducing ineffective treatments
Key references	Rogers (2003); Berwick (2003)

Service Innovation

Service innovation is a form of innovation that focuses on creating value through novel service delivery methods. In the healthcare context, this means questioning accessibility, efficiency, and personalized care, often, but not only, through harnessing digital solutions (Willie, 2024). Examples of service innovation include telemedicine platforms for remote consultations (Haleem et al., 2021), patient-centered medical homes that establish coordinated care models (Duan-Porter et al., 2022), virtual reality therapy (Bateni et al., 2024; Tokgöz et al., 2022) and Health Information Exchanges that enable patient information sharing across providers (Tiase et al., 2020).

Telemedicine (or even more so a phone call) is one way to avoid emissions, in particular those related to transportation, although the extent to which this is profitable from an environmental perspective is very dependent on the context in which it is used (urban vs rural, dense vs non-dense areas…) (Pickard Strange et al., 2023; Purohit et al., 2021; Ravindrane & Patel, 2022). This represents a quantity of 830 million kg of carbon dioxide emissions primarily through reduced transportation in a total of 50 studies (Berger et al., 2025).[3] Carbon savings related to transportation ranged from 95 to 99% of the impacts in some cases, from 0.70–372 kg CO2e per consultation (Purohit et al., 2021; Ravindrane & Patel, 2022). At the meso level, some organizations avoided thousands of metric tons of greenhouse gases in 2021 through telemedicine(Morcillo Serra et al., 2022; Thiel et al., 2023). The benefits of the other forms of service innovation (patient-centered medical homes, virtual reality therapy, health information exchanges) are much less documented from the environmental perspective. It is still possible to find traces and infer possible environmental benefits. For instance, patient-centered medical homes initiatives, a model aimed at "improving healthcare quality, decreasing cost, and enhancing the experience of both patients and providers" (Arend et al., 2012) were associated with reduced ambulatory care-sensitive emergency department visits(Rosenthal et al., 2013), and noted a 4.2% reduction in total healthcare spending (Sinaiko et al., 2017). Literature on Health Information Exchanges (HIEs) do not explicitly discuss environmental impacts as primary goal but mention reduction of paper usage or unnecessary medical procedures (Hersh et al., 2015; Menachemi et al., 2018). Electronic health records (EHRs) enable service coordination that significantly reduces unnecessary repeated laboratory tests (hemoglobin A1c, vitamin B12, lipid panels), cutting both costs and environmental impact through better information management (Molero et al., 2021). Implementation barriers include a fee-for-service which is more rewarded than community-based care, organizational silos that fragment coordination for sustainability project which are cross-sector by nature and professional hierarchies devalue primary care and prevention (see Appendix E for more details on the barriers).

A Telemedicine Program

During and after the COVID-19 pandemic, a healthcare center has conducted over 2 million virtual visits between 2020–2023, saving 17,000 metric tons of greenhouse gas emissions in 2021 alone (primarily through eliminated patient and provider travel since each teleconsultation saved an average of 8.5 kg CO_2e compared to in-person visits). This program also improved access for rural patients, reduced patient costs by $150–300, all of this while maintaining clinical quality scores equivalent to in-person care. The service model permanently transformed care delivery across 15 clinical specialties.

Service innovation at a glance	
Definition	New ways of delivering and organizing care services through technology-enabled models
Key characteristics	Reorganization of care delivery methods Integration of technology with service design Focus on accessibility and patient experience
Contexts	Outpatient clinics, telehealth platforms, community health centers, home care services

(continued)

[3] This was discussed in an article (Brulé & Pichon, 2025).

(continued)

Service innovation at a glance	
Sustainability strengths	Reduction of patient travel through remote consultations Reduction of facility energy use through distributed care Reduction of infrastructure needs through virtualization
Sustainability limitations	Digital infrastructure energy consumption and e-waste Rebound effects from increased service accessibility Requires robust internet connectivity infrastructure
Barriers to implementation	Fee-for-service more rewarded than community-based care Organizational silos fragment coordination Professional hierarchies devalue primary care and prevention
Relationship to other innovation types	Technological Innovation (e.g., telemedicine platforms) Organizational Innovation (e.g., integrated care networks) Process Innovation (e.g., streamlined patient pathways)
Key indicators	Patient travel avoided (km not traveled via telemedicine) Facility energy savings (kWh from distributed care) Carbon emissions per consultation (kg CO_2e comparison)
Examples	Telemedicine consultations reducing travel emissions Mobile health clinics reaching underserved areas Home-based dialysis programs
Key references	Gallouj and Djellal (2005); Gallouj and Weinstein (1997)

Socio-organizational Innovation

If technology is only part of the answer as acknowledged in the previous chapter, this means that a lot can be gained within the "folds of the social"(Lahire, 2019). Therefore, reducing environmental impacts of the healthcare sector requires organizational innovations (top-down) and social innovations (bottom-up) that transform care organization, role distributions, and professional practices.

Before entering the different folds above-mentioned, it is important to grasp the multi-scalar dynamics of care innovation. Building upon the theories of Van de Ven's process theory of innovation and Geels (Multi-Level Perspective (MLP), we can try to see how micro, meso, and macro are interconnected (Geels, 2002; Van de Ven et al.,

1999). Although the micro-meso are the scales of interests here, it is also important to understand how the macro is constituted, since it is also constitutive and typically influences back the two other levels through construction of norms, institutions, guidelines, etc. In line with systems theory, one can recognize that healthcare is a complex adaptive system with emergent properties that cannot be understood through linear, unidimensional approaches (Meadows, 2015).

In *micro-level* niches, radical innovations and experiments emerge, for instance, with a new product or a new process. If successful, this innovation can expand to *meso-level* regimes (e.g., clinical routines, procurement standards, hospital infrastructure). Wider adoption is done at the *macro-level* landscape, where other forces are in action such as defined societal trends and pressures, climate change and carbon-reducing targets, as well as pandemics. At that level, *learning health systems*[4] provide a comprehensive framework for coordinating organizational structures in order to advance toward environmental sustainability through systematic monitoring of the environmental impacts and well-coordinated leadership (Barber et al., 2024). Transitions occur when landscape-level pressures regimes, allowing niche innovations to challenge or reconfigure them. However, the meso level is not just a passive interface; it is rather a site of organizational inertia, adoption, and contestation. Van de Ven's model highlights the fact that innovation trajectories often involve setbacks, reorientations, and multiple competing visions. This model shows the cumulative effect from marginal niches to broader healthcare regime change. These complex dynamics of sustainable innovation echo the writings of Simmel, Merton, or the Schumpeterian representation of innovation from the marginal innovations to the imitation by a bunch of followers to a stabilization into new rules of the game (Fig. 4.2).

Process Innovation

Process innovation refers to the implementation of new or significantly improved production or delivery methods. In the healthcare sector, it is generally seen as a way to improve the efficiency of the care process by translating knowledge into improved healthcare products and procedures (Collins & Dempsey, 2019; Omachonu & Einspruch, 2010). Process innovation can reduce environmental impacts by saving material, by reducing CO_2 emissions or by improving recycling (Benzidia et al., 2024; Swałek & Steinerowska-Streb, 2023). This includes avoiding unnecessary tests as in the example: "no laboratory tests apart from blood grouping and cross-matching were requested. However, we used radiological investigations extensively and avoided unnecessary surgical interventions" (Deshpande et al., 2007). Choosing Wisely campaigns target overuse of tests providing no clinical benefit (or sometimes even harm), while also generating environmental harm although this is not often

[4] An environment that integrates data, science, and technology continuously into routine clinical practices.

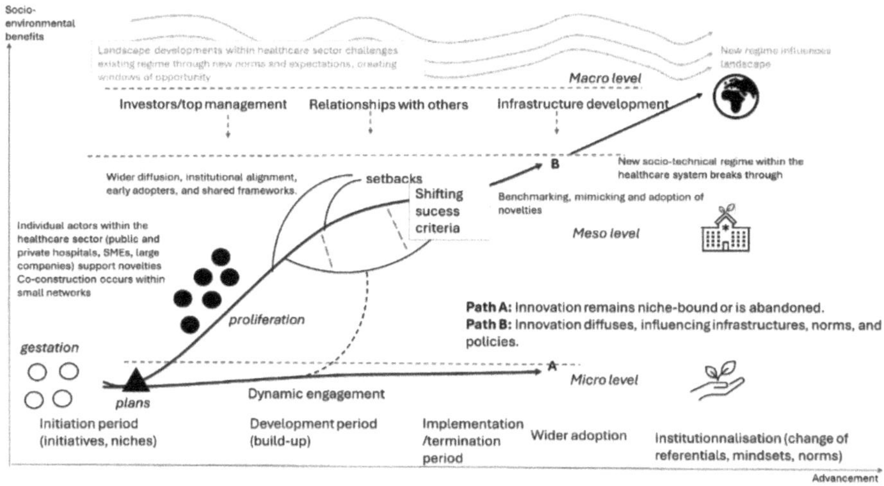

Fig. 4.2 Multi-scalar spiral of care innovation (adapted from van de Ven and Geels)

the primary concern (Charmillot et al., 2025). Active interventions targeting clinicians show 65% success rates versus 13% for guideline dissemination alone(Cliff et al., 2021). Reducing intravenous antibiotics when oral alternatives suffice, minimizing greenhouse gas-intensive inhalers, and eliminating unnecessary daily blood tests (Bounoure et al., s. d.; J. F. Davies et al., 2024; Gaudreau-Simard et al., 2025). Lean Healthcare Management supports these objectives through process optimization (Crema & Verbano, 2017). Complementary strategies including energy management programs and surgical waste reduction through kit redesign demonstrate both environmental benefits (234 metric tons CO_2 reduction, 22% waste decrease) and cost savings (de Ridder et al., 2022; Wormer et al., 2013). Some changes at the macro level can show large impacts as for instance shifting from atorvastatin to generic simvastatin in the United Kingdom was one way to save billions of pounds and diminish impacts through simpler process and shorter supply chain.[5]

Medical devices and consumables can reduce environmental impacts of items such as surgical gowns, ureteroscopes, anesthetic drug tray through reusability, with reusable devices demonstrating 40–66% lower emissions compared to single-use alternatives (Keil et al., 2023; Lam et al., 2023). However, parts of the environmental benefits of the reusability are overshadowed by sterilization methods, which can account for up to 90% of reprocessed device greenhouse gas emissions (Leiden et al., 2020).

Clinical guidelines, which have emerged in the healthcare sector in the 1970s, driven by quality concerns, legal liability, and the evidence-based medicine movement, are one promising way to bring significant changes vis-à-vis sustainability. Defined as "systematically developed statements to assist practitioner and patient

[5] Although not prescribing statin when not needed is the most impactful measure to reduce statin-related environmental impact (Auer et al., 2014).

decisions about appropriate health care for specific clinical circumstances" (Field & Lohr, 1990), they are designed to standardize care pathways. From a sustainability perspective, although encouraging (reduce greenhouse gas emissions by eliminating unnecessary procedures, streamlining diagnostic pathways, and standardizing waste management practices(Braithwaite et al., 2024; Townend & Cheeseman, 2005), guidelines remain for the moment largely environmentally blind. However, as Khan et al. (2023) demonstrate with respiratory guidelines, even when sustainable alternatives exist, they remain absent from prescribing protocols, like for instance dry powder inhalers generating 90–95% less emissions than pressurized metered-dose inhalers (pMDIs), which generate approximately 28 kg CO_2-equivalent emissions (equivalent to a 300 km car journey) per unit. On the other hand, guidelines tend to encode unnecessary complexity over sustainable alternatives (Govindarajan & Ramamurti, 2011). Standardizing surgical procedures and using fossil-free textiles can significantly reduce carbon footprints in operating theaters (Lindskog & Männer, 2019). Interventions that reduce unnecessary cardiac tests through alerts based on electronic health records and educational feedback to clinicians achieve 10–17 ton CO_2e reductions annually. Evidence-based perioperative pathways like Enhanced Recovery After Surgery (ERAS) and same-day discharge protocols reduce resource consumption while improving clinical outcomes (MacNeill et al., 2024). Implementation barriers include temporal architecture of urgency, resource-intensive protocols and organizational silos which impede cross-functional authority (see Appendix E for more details on the barriers).

Enhanced Recovery After Surgery (ERAS) Protocol

Enhanced Recovery After Surgery (ERAS) protocols were implemented and standardized in a large European hospital for 8 surgical specialties. The protocol resulted in improved patients' outcomes, reducing average hospital stays from 7 to 4 days for colorectal surgery with patients experiencing fewer complications, and faster recovery, while also saving 4′200 euros per surgical episode and improving environmental footprint by reducing lab tests by 35%, switching from IV antibiotic to oral use whenever possible and using standardized surgical kits, thereby saving 234 tons of CO_2 per year.

Process innovation at a glance	
Definition	New workflows, protocols, pathways, and operational methods that improve efficiency and coordination
Key characteristics	Redesign of operational workflows and procedures Focus on efficiency and waste reduction Requires organizational change management
Contexts	Hospital operations, supply chain management, clinical pathways, administrative services

(continued)

(continued)

Process innovation at a glance	
Sustainability strengths	Reduction of material waste through lean methodologies Reduction of energy use through optimized operations Reduction of redundant procedures and resource consumption
Sustainability limitations	Risk of increased throughput driving higher overall consumption Focus on efficiency may overlook broader environmental impacts Implementation requires energy and resources for transition
Barriers to implementation	Temporal architecture of urgency Resource-intensive protocols Organizational silos impede cross-functional authority
Relationship to other innovation types	Organizational Innovation (e.g., governance structures enabling new processes) Technological Innovation (e.g., digital tools automating workflows) Business Model Innovation (e.g., value-based care pathways)
Key indicators	Supply waste reduction (% decrease in unused supplies) Procedure standardization (% variance reduction) Resource utilization rate (% improvement in efficiency)
Examples	Lean hospital operations reducing supply waste Just-in-time inventory systems minimizing overstock Standardized clinical pathways reducing unnecessary tests
Key references	Hammer and Champy (1993), Davenport (1993)

Organizational Innovation

Organizational innovation describes the process of developing and implementing new ideas within an organizational context to improve organizational functioning. This bridging aspect of organizational innovation is the reason why it is studied by various disciplines (business, economics, engineering, public administration, see Damanpour, 2017). Bouwen and Fry (1991) define it as "the development and implementation of new ideas by people who engage over time in transactions with others within an institutional order", highlighting its interactive nature. Organizational innovations range all the way from small adjustments to deep structural changes, which can entail environmental, social or economic benefits of different magnitude (Sullivan et al.,

2023) found that operating room interventions could achieve annual cost savings ranging from \$873 to \$694,141, and a reduction of regulated medical waste of up to 30%. Life cycle assessment can support management decision-making by providing detailed information of the environmental impacts in order to foster organizational changes (Seifert et al., 2021).

Creating a "green culture" in healthcare can hardly be done overnight; it requires leaders to distill sustainability into clinical choices, governance frameworks, and staff practices (Porter-O'Grady & Malloch, 2010a, 2010b). If creating a culture cannot be done (or undone) easily, organizational innovations can tackle most actionable spheres such as purchasing practices, waste management, energy efficiency and distill sustainability within authority structures, accountability and work routines (Fadda, 2020). As far as the routines are concerned, key players can make it possible to turn abstract guidelines or sustainability goals into concrete actions by mobilizing resources, persuading colleagues, and embodying the credibility needed.

At the inter-organizational level, innovation can take the form of associations or networks with, for instance, professional societies increasingly erect sustainability principles and standards, embedding environmental priorities into practical guidelines. Or, they can act on a specific goal, as, for instance, groups of hospitals deciding to collectively demand greener products, using leverage over manufacturers, thereby accelerating changes within the supply chain. Coalitions can include a couple of regional hospitals or international networks. For instance, Health Care Without Harm formed a global coalition of 28 organizations, establishing the Global Green and Healthy Hospitals community in 2010 for networking and peer learning (Clinton, 2018). Organizational innovation requires some tools to facilitate change, such as design thinking instruments. In the Nordic healthcare context, collaborative foresight workshops were used to engage diverse stakeholders (health industries, providers, regional authorities, universities, clusters, NGOs, and professional consortia) using systemic design methods combined with the Three Horizons framework to enable cross-sectoral dialogue and shared decision-making (Pereno & Eriksson, 2020). However, inter-organizational networks can also reproduce inertia if they converge on lowest-common-denominator standards that satisfy all members but lack transformative ambition (Ulhøi & Ulhøi, 2009).

Engagement and well-being can play a key role in terms of organizational innovation to reduce environmental impacts. Since job satisfaction is key for workforce stability and motivation (Hoxha et al., 2024), cultures which integrated inclusivity, psychological safety, and recognition achieve better outcomes at the individual and the team level (Ahmed et al., 2021; Wang et al., 2025). Implementation barriers include voluntary reporting, which can lead to greenwashing; silos, which fragment cross-sectoral authority; and power dynamics and resource-intensive protocols (see Appendix E for more details on the barriers).

Hospital's Sustainability Transformation

A hospital in Africa made significant organizational changes through strong political leadership, supportive government policies, and dedicated funding. The hospital restructured governance to integrate sustainability alongside, establishing a "Green Leadership Committee" reporting directly to executive management. Concrete changes included appointing sustainability champions in each department, integrating environmental metrics into the performance evaluation framework and implementing staff training programs. This led to a reduction in energy consumption of 50%, a decrease in water usage of 50%, a decrease in the production of medical waste of 30% and recycling rate going from 15 to 65% over 5 years.

Organizational innovation at a glance	
Definition	New structures, governance systems, and institutional coordination mechanisms that reshape how healthcare organizations operate
Key characteristics	Restructuring of institutional arrangements and hierarchies Changes in governance and decision-making systems Focus on inter-organizational collaboration and coordination
Contexts	Healthcare systems, hospital networks, public health authorities, multi-stakeholder partnerships
Sustainability strengths	Reduction of duplicated services through coordination Reduction of administrative overhead through streamlined governance Reduction of resource fragmentation through integrated planning
Sustainability limitations	Organizational restructuring consumes time and resources Increased complexity may require additional coordination infrastructure Resistance to change can delay environmental improvements
Barriers to implementation	Voluntary reporting & greenwashing Silos fragment authority Power dynamics Health-as-a-business view
Relationship to other innovation types	Process Innovation (e.g., new workflows require organizational alignment) Business Model Innovation (e.g., governance structures enable new financing) Social Innovation (e.g., community partnerships reshape institutional roles)

(continued)

(continued)

Organizational innovation at a glance	
Key indicators	Waste diversion rate (% of waste recycled/avoided) Procurement sustainability score (% green purchasing compliance) Energy/water consumption per patient (reduction from baseline)
Examples	Integrated care networks reducing redundant testing Shared service centers consolidating support functions Multi-hospital purchasing consortia leveraging collective power
Key references	Lam (2006); Damanpour (2017)

Social Innovation

Social innovation is a process of change emerging from creative recombination of existing assets (equipment, network, facilities) to achieve social goals through bottom-up, community-driven initiatives (Manzini, 2014). The bottom-up approach means that the innovations stem from people (in this context employees, patients, caregivers…) directly involved in solving social problems (Castro-Arce & Vanclay, 2020). It is community-driven in the sense that it is driven by community needs rather than by market forces (Moulaert et al., 2013a, 2013b). From the healthcare perspective, local actors can drive health innovations more effectively than top-down approaches(Halpaap et al., 2020), increasing accountability and sustainability (Daniel & Jenner, 2022). For instance, social prescribing services decrease the environmental impacts of the healthcare sector by reducing secondary-care referrals and offering lower-carbon alternatives such as cognitive behavioral therapy (Maughan et al., 2016). Community-based social innovations developed bottom-up by local beneficiaries create sustainable healthcare solutions by empowering communities (Mdleleni & Velapi, 2022). The initiatives of *Housing first* (Un chez soi d'abord (France), INSP! (Denmark)) make it possible to imagine an ethical, alternative path to resource-consuming hospitals by keeping patients at home (Bauer et al., 2016). Interdisciplinary grassroot movements led by sometimes informal leaders can rapidly advance environmental stewardship through waste diversion, energy efficiency, and green purchasing practices (Herechuk et al., 2010).

Social innovation emerges as a shift from a unidirectional model in which physicians "provide" and patients "receive", toward a reconfiguration of the relationships between professionals, patients, and families, which favors co-production and deliberative decisions. While patients are increasingly involved in shaping their own care pathways, families and caregivers are recognized not just as auxiliaries, but as co-actors in care delivery (for instance, the *patient partenaire*("patient partner") at Geneva University Hospitals, among others). Value co-creation through stakeholder engagement has not only benefits in terms of health outcomes but also in terms of sustainable social change in healthcare delivery(Ahmed et al., 2020). Implementation barriers include the marginalization of bottom-up grassroots solutions and community health and a hierarchy of professions which devalue community health work (see Appendix E for more details on the barriers).

Community Health Worker Model

A bottom-up program in South-East Asia has trained community health workers to provide primary care services, conduct health education, and facilitate hospital access for needy patients, enabling 40% of previously excluded patients to access hospital care without direct payment. At the social level, equity and wider health coverage was obtained. At the environmental level, reduced transportation through local care delivery, minimized hospital infrastructure through primary prevention and sustainable behavior change were achieved for a small annual participation ($15 per capita annually, 95% less than hospital-based care, while improving maternal and child health outcomes across 78 rural districts).

Social innovation at a glance	
Definition	Bottom-up, community-driven solutions addressing social needs and health inequities through collective action
Key characteristics	Grassroots and participatory approaches Addresses social determinants of health Emphasis on empowerment and community ownership
Contexts	Community health centers, non-profit organizations, patient advocacy groups, local health initiatives
Sustainability strengths	Reduction of healthcare demand through prevention and social support Reduction of resource intensity through community-based solutions Reduction of institutional overhead through peer support networks
Sustainability limitations	Limited scalability without institutional support Dependence on volunteer capacity and community resources Environmental impact often secondary to social objectives
Barriers to implementation	Bottom-up grassroots solutions and community health marginalized Professional hierarchies devalue community health work

(continued)

(continued)

Social innovation at a glance	
Relationship to other innovation types	Organizational Innovation (e.g., new partnerships with community groups) Service Innovation (e.g., community-based care delivery) Cultural Innovation (e.g., shifting values toward collective health)
Key indicators	Healthcare demand reduction (% fewer secondary-care referrals) Community resource mobilization (volunteer hours, peer support) Institutional cost avoidance ($ saved per capita)
Examples	Community gardens promoting nutrition and mental health Peer support networks reducing hospital readmissions Time banks for elderly care reducing institutionalization
Key references	Moulaert et al., (2013a, 2013b), Manzini (2014)

Business Model Innovation

The question of business model innovation can be handled either from a more organizational perspective (e.g., circular economy, industrial ecology) or from a more technological perspective. Both perspectives come with their promises and challenges.

Circular economy business models represent one way for reducing environmental impacts at the meso level in healthcare. These can take the form of sustainable procurement strategies or dynamic business model redesign. Some authors have developed frameworks such as a five-level circular economy framework with quantifiable cost and CO_2 emission formulas for reuse versus single-use medical devices (Moshawih et al., 2025). Business models such as Dynamic Business Modeling for Sustainability (Cosenz et al., 2024) or articulated around product lifetime extension (Ertz & Patrick, 2020) can reduce waste in energy, water, and medical supplies while improving cost-effectiveness. However, proper implementation of business model requires budget allocation, strategic commitment, and transformational leadership, factors that are unevenly distributed across healthcare systems (Aboueid et al., 2023).

FinTech development can facilitate the healthcare sector's transition to low-carbon economies (Li et al., 2024). To some authors, the convergence of financial technology and health technology enables more efficient healthcare delivery through Fintech (blockchain technology) potentially reducing the sector's overall ecological footprint (Cambaza, 2023). New business models can integrate environmental performance in global performance frameworks (Hensher & McGain, 2020). Business model innovation introduces new ways of financing and organizing healthcare economics (such as value-based care, subscription medicine, bundled payments) (Alami et al., 2023). Implementation barriers include the absence of polluter-pays principles which externalizes environmental costs, fragmented decision-making across finance, clinical and sustainability departments, and performance metrics ignore environmental outcomes (see Appendix E for more details on the barriers).

Other authors consider the pros and cons of technological adoption in business model, arguing that the environmental cost of the infrastructure will add another layer of complexity from a sustainability perspective (Rønn et al., 2023).

A New Value-Based Care Model

A primary care organization in North America dedicated to elderly patients has reorganized its business model around value-based care, where the focus is on health outcomes over costs. Physicians are paid based on patient health improvements and not on visit volume or act, thereby favoring preventive care, minimally invasive approaches, and reduced hospitalizations. This shift in the *lens* used to observe quality resulted in a 50% reduction in hospital admissions, 40% fewer emergency department visits, and improved clinical outcomes for chronic disease management. The model demonstrated profitability, generating $450 million annual revenue across more than 100 centers. On the environmental side, this led to an estimated 9–20% decrease in carbon emissions per patient through shifting care to lower-intensity primary care settings and reducing unnecessary procedures and tests.

Business model innovation at a glance	
Definition	New approaches to financing and organizing healthcare economics that reshape value creation and delivery
Key characteristics	Redesign of revenue streams and cost structures Changes in value propositions and stakeholder relationships Focus on financial sustainability and economic viability
Contexts	Healthcare systems, insurance companies, hospital management, payment reform initiatives
Sustainability strengths	Reduction of overtreatment through value-based payment models Reduction of waste through aligned financial incentives Reduction of resource use through preventive care economics
Sustainability limitations	Profit motives may conflict with environmental priorities Short-term financial pressures limit long-term sustainability investments Market-based approaches may neglect ecological externalities

(continued)

(continued)

Business model innovation at a glance	
Barriers to implementation	Absence of polluter-pays principles externalizes environmental costs Fragmented decision-making across finance/clinical/sustainability departments Performance metrics ignore environmental outcomes
Relationship to other innovation types	Organizational Innovation (e.g., governance enabling new financing) Process Innovation (e.g., new payment models drive workflow changes) Service Innovation (e.g., subscription-based care models)
Key indicators	Preventive care rate (% patients in prevention programs) Overtreatment reduction (% decrease in low-value care) Value per resource unit (health outcomes per $ or kg CO_2e)
Examples	Capitation payment reducing unnecessary procedures Pay-for-performance linking quality to environmental metrics Shared savings programs incentivizing resource efficiency
Key references	Chesbrough (2010), Osterwalder and Pigneur (2013)

Paradigmatic Innovation

Paradigmatic innovation operates at several levels. Frugal innovation shows that resource constraints can drive not just cheaper solutions but more robust and resilient ones. Cultural innovation can take the form of shifts in professional norms, institutional practices, and collective values that redefine what constitutes good care. At the foundational level, imaginaries represent the archaeologies of meaning that determine what is thinkable, desirable, and legitimate in healthcare.

Frugal Innovation

According to UNICEF Innocenti data, the UK and USA among the lowest in child well-being across 21 rich countries, despite advanced and expensive health systems. This paradox reveals that technological abundance does not guarantee better outcomes. On top of primary prevention and health promotion which are lagging behind in these two countries, particularly in the USA (Arie, 2012), quality of care often depends more on relevance and accessibility than on complexity. This is where frugal innovation ("Doing more with less") can intervene. It is often developed in constrained contexts where natural or human resources are scarce and logistics dysfunctional or in crises like Darfur, where health interventions must be agile and immediately impactful (Brown, 2007): use of mosquito net for hernia repairs in Ghana, insulin storage pot in Nort-East Africa, Toyota-inspired mode of performing cataract or heart surgery, low-cost dialysis (Table 4.1). Far from a "technological bricolage" (Lévi-Strauss, 1962), it is a novel way of adapting to ones' environment. The benefits are often formulated in economic terms. At Aravind, cataract surgery, the costs for an operation including intraocular lenses and associated care are in the range of $11.50 to $100 compared to an average of $3,542 for the same procedure in the United States. Coronary bypass surgery at Narayana Health costs around $2,100, while U.S. prices range from $76,000 to $342,000. Angioplasty, knee and hip replacements, and cancer radiotherapy follow similar patterns, with Indian prices ranging from 2 to 12% of U.S. costs. Similarly, LifeSpring Hospitals provides maternity care at approximately $120 for vaginal deliveries and $300 for cesarean sections, compared to an average of $8,802 in the U.S. Naryanya Health provides a typical heart surgery for $2,100, tens of thousands less than in the United States. Although 60% of pediatric surgeries are provided for free, Naranya is a profitable company with a market valuation over a billion dollars. At Deccan Hospital, peritoneal dialysis (including diagnostics, medication, and hospitalization) costs about $8,200 per year, compared to $89,000 typically spent on hemodialysis in the United States. Most of these examples come from India, which has emerged as a global laboratory for frugal innovation in healthcare. Only part of this had to do with income differences (Ramdorai & Herstatt, 2015). Low-cost portable ultrasound machine was developed to be of use for low and middle-income countries (e.g., GE electric or (Chavignon et al., 2022). But it could also be formulated in environmental terms. For instance, a clay pot costing $1–2 and generating 1–3 kg CO_2e achieves the same therapeutic outcome as refrigeration equipment costing $250-$500 and generating 80–100 kg CO_2, although arguably the level of apparent control is lower. This 100-fold difference in both cost and environmental impact reveals how our assumptions about "appropriate technology" often favor complexity over effectiveness, global supply chains over local solutions, and energy intensity over resource efficiency.

While frugal innovation often produces technoproductive outputs (devices, processes), its constitutive core is cultural: the embrace of sufficiency over maximalism, accessibility over sophistication, and "good enough" over "cutting-edge". As Radjou et al. (2012) note, frugal innovation "is not just about redesigning products; it involves rethinking entire business models and reorienting organizational cultures" (p. 4), a fundamentally paradigmatic, not merely technical, transformation. Or as Kiefer (2022) points out, "always use the reflection less is more, but where less translates in a radical form of intelligent economy". This means that to achieve frugal innovation, it is not sufficient to simply use less material or energy or to change procedures. It is necessary to change the mindset to a mindset of "good enough" (Brulé et al., 2026), one that can result not only in a decrease of energy and material input, but also of greater robustness, national sovereignty and least exposure to global disruptions in the supply chain or wars.

Implementation barriers include a cultural paradigm equating complexity with quality and "low-tech" solutions perceived as regression, professional identity related to mastery of hyper-tech environment and a fee-for-service rewards resource intensity over material simplicity (see Appendix E for more details on the barriers) (Fig. 4.3).

Other forms of frugal innovation are displayed in Appendix E. Crucially, what distinguishes frugal innovation is not only its material sobriety but its epistemology. By focusing on core health needs and using light infrastructures that may not be sustainable in unstable environments, frugal innovation creates an ethics of care that goes beyond traditional models. This approach connects with value-based care principles (Porter & Teisberg, 2006).

Frugal innovation at a glance	
Definition	Affordable, resource-constrained solutions emphasizing simplicity, accessibility, and doing more with less
Key characteristics	Low-cost and resource-efficient design Emphasizes affordability and accessibility Often developed in or for resource-limited settings
Contexts	Low-resource settings, community clinics, humanitarian healthcare, rural and remote areas
Sustainability strengths	Reduction of material use through minimalist design Reduction of energy consumption through low-tech approaches Reduction of supply chain complexity through local production

(continued)

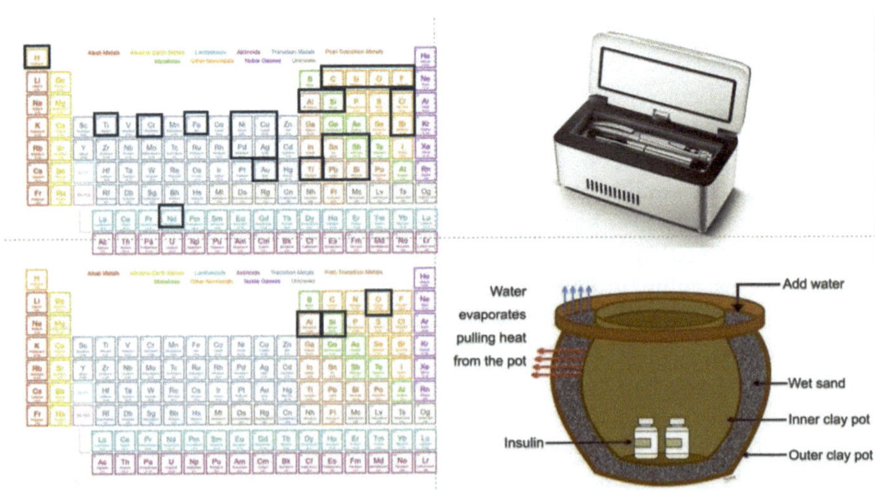

Fig. 4.3 Insulin refrigerator versus zeerpot

(continued)

Frugal innovation at a glance	
Sustainability limitations	May lack durability leading to premature replacement Limited standardization can hinder quality control Scalability challenges without compromising frugal principles
Barriers to implementation	Cultural paradigm equating complexity with quality and "low-tech" solutions perceived as regression professional identity related to mastery of hyper-tech environment fee-for-service rewards resource intensity over material simplicity
Relationship to other innovation types	Social Innovation (e.g., community-based healthcare solutions) Technological Innovation (e.g., simplified diagnostic devices) Service Innovation (e.g., mobile clinics with minimal infrastructure)
Key indicators	Cost per outcome ($ per QALY or cure) Material intensity (kg per treatment/device) Local production rate (% components sourced locally)
Examples	Paper-based diagnostic tools reducing equipment needs Gravity-fed drip irrigation for medical gardens Reusable cloth surgical supplies in low-resource settings
Key references	Radjou et al. (2012), Bhatti and Ventresca (2013)

Portable Ultrasound: Reverse Innovation in Diagnostics

Initially developed for low- and middle-income countries where traditional hospital-grade ultrasound systems were too expensive and required stable electricity infrastructure, portable devices simplified the technology by reducing elemental complexity from approximately 25 elements (advanced imaging chips, multiple specialized transducers, high-resolution displays requiring rare earth metals and complex electronics) to approximately 15 elements through streamlined design. Rather than remaining confined to resource-constrained settings, portable ultrasound achieved "reverse innovation", adoption in high-income countries where its material simplicity translated into other advantages (immediate point-of-care availability, eliminating patient transport to radiology suites).

Cultural Innovation

We have seen that healthcare embraced the theme of sustainability after other sectors. This can be attributed to a "cultural lag" (Ogburn, 1922). This cultural lag in healthcare can be understood as the time gap between the broader societal recognition of environmental challenges and the healthcare sector's integration of sustainability principles into its core mission, practices, and professional identity. It is in that sense cultural. But as we saw, this gap is currently being filled by an intense pressure to do better both from the organizations, as seen in the previous chapter and from healthcare workers themselves. This is being done also at larger, cultural level through cultural innovations. Although particularly fragmented (Pozzo et al., 2020), the landscape of cultural innovation usually depicts a collective process whereby new ideas, practices, and knowledge that "enhance survival and adaptation within diverse environments. It is characterized by the accumulation of culturally transmittable information that influences cognition, affect, and behavior" (Halford, 2020).

If cultural innovation is so fragmented, it is also because cultures are so heterogeneous in general and in the healthcare sector is no exception; from public hospitals to private clinics or ambulatory care, from long-term care to community health centers, the places where care is delivered are as diverse as the variety of the cultures of the professions who compose them: physicians, nurses, physiotherapists, pharmacists, administrators. Organizational culture is key to fostering innovation and sustainability in healthcare (Porter-O'Grady & Malloch, 2010a, 2010b). But as we shall see, there are brakes in the culture of the organizations, of these professions and of the care as it is currently thought that make changes difficult. Modern systems tend to "medicalize" everyday life, turning normal variations into clinical conditions. Frugal and cultural innovations offer a corrective by focusing on essential functions rather than technological escalation, reducing complexity while preserving clinical relevance.

Imaginaries

Imaginaries are usually the most macro part in systems innovation. They are the recipiendaries and the producers of collective representations. Far from being soft and abstract, they are the driving forces that shape institutions, categories, and the rationalities that structure social life. For Castoriadis, the imaginary is the collective force that creates and forms the symbolic structures of a society or a part of it. Healthcare's dominant rationality, which relies on efficiency, cleanliness, and control, is not existing *sui generis*, but it is produced through such an imaginary.

"the ways in which we know and represent the world (both nature and society) are inseparable from the ways in which we choose to live in it" (Jasanoff, 2004, p. 2).

What appears as neutral technical necessity is actually the result of historically contingent meaning-making processes. In their system based on 4 types of innovations, Tidd and Bessant (2014) challenge the underlying mental models, like redefining health systems around prevention and sustainability rather than acute intervention. This naturally means that as for any systemic thinking they are also related to meso, organizational changes, and micro individual considerations such as professional identities. Implementation barriers include a feeling of medical omnipotence, professional identity which can feel threatened by challenging norms and immediate patient needs favored upon long-term environmental harm (see Appendix E for more details on the barriers).

Cultural innovation at a glance	
Definition	Shifts in values, norms, mindsets, and behaviors that transform how healthcare professionals and patients understand and practice care
Key characteristics	Changes in beliefs, attitudes, and professional culture Requires long-term behavioral and normative shifts Often invisible but foundational for other innovations
Contexts	Medical education, professional training, healthcare organizations, patient communities
Sustainability strengths	Reduction of overconsumption through changed professional norms Reduction of resistance to environmental innovations Reduction of wasteful practices through behavioral change
Sustainability limitations	Slow and difficult to implement and measure Resistance from established professional cultures Requires sustained effort without immediate tangible results
Barriers to implementation	Medical omnipotence Professional identity threatened by challenging norms Immediate patient needs favored upon long-term environmental harm
Relationship to other innovation types	Organizational Innovation (e.g., culture shapes institutional practices) Social Innovation (e.g., community values influence care norms) Clinical Innovation (e.g., cultural shifts enable practice changes)
Key indicators	Professional behavior change (% adoption of sustainable practices) Prescribing patterns (% reduction in unnecessary medications) End-of-life care intensity (% reduction in futile interventions)

(continued)

(continued)

Cultural innovation at a glance	
Examples	Deprescribing culture reducing unnecessary medications Green healthcare champions promoting environmental awareness Patient empowerment movements reducing medicalization
Key references	DiMaggio (1997), Schein (2010)

"Good Enough Death" Guidelines in Intensive Care Medicine
A European society of Intensive Care Medicine issued sustainability-focused clinical guidelines challenging the cultural imperative to "do everything possible" at end-of-life. The Top 5 Smarter Medicine recommendations include: "Do not pursue intensive care for people with severe risk of dying without discussing therapeutic goals with patients or their representatives". This cultural innovation redefines "good care" from maximal intervention to appropriate intervention aligned with patient values. Implementation at a large European hospital reduced ICU admissions for terminal patients by 25%, decreased resource consumption in the final 2 weeks of life by 40%, and improved patient and family satisfaction scores. The paradigm shift, from "more is better" to "good enough", saves approximately 18 tons CO_2e per 100 end-of-life patients while honoring dignity and autonomy.

What Innovation to Reduce the Environmental Impacts of the Healthcare Sector?

The list of the 9 forms of innovations is summarized in Table 4.2.

We have seen that there are many ways to define, to rank, and characterize the different forms of innovation. Beyond the idiosyncratic character of each type of innovation, it is important to understand in the context of this work that they carry different forms of novelty (although we saw earlier that it depends on the perspective of who judges it) and different degrees of impact on the environment. In the Fig. 4.4, we use two axes: first, to what degree innovations are incremental or radical and second, to what degree they are based on a low or high amount of resources. This categorization is based on ranking and comparison of the different types of innovation. The positioning resulted from comparative evaluation of innovation, based on literature, criteria of resource intensity (material/energy inputs), and degree of departure from established practice (incremental versus systemic transformation). Naturally, it faces some limitations. The first one has to do with the categorization itself. The categories are less watertight to another than what can be seen on the

Table 4.2 Synthetic table of the nine forms of innovation

Innovation Type	Category	Description	Key References
Technological Innovation	Technoproductive	New devices, equipment, materials, and digital tools	Schumpeter (1942); Dosi (1982); Freeman & Soete (2007)
Clinical Innovation	Technoproductive	New diagnostic, therapeutic, and treatment approaches	Rogers (1995); Berwick (2003)
Service Innovation	Technoproductive	New ways of delivering and organizing care services through technology	Gallouj and Djellal (2005); Gallouj and Weinstein (1997)
Business Model Innovation	Socio-organizational	New approaches to financing and organizing healthcare economics	Chesbrough (2010); Osterwalder and Pigneur (2010)
Organizational Innovation	Socio-organizational	New structures, governance systems, and institutional coordination	Lam (2005); Damanpour (2017)
Process Innovation	Socio-organizational	New workflows, protocols, pathways, and operational methods	Hammer and Champy (1993); Davenport (1993)
Social Innovation	Socio-organizational	Bottom-up, community-driven solutions addressing social needs	Moulaert et al., (2013a, 2013b); Manzini (2014)
Cultural Innovation	Paradigmatic	Shifts in values, norms, mindsets, and behaviors	DiMaggio (1997); Schein (2010)
Frugal Innovation	Paradigmatic	Affordable, resource-constrained solutions emphasizing simplicity and accessibility	Radjou et al. (2012); Bhatti and Ventresca (2013)

graph. Many innovations can fit in several categories, and in that context, one must do the sometimes difficult exercise of deciding which form of innovation it is the most related to and "purify" it accordingly. Yet, the reality is as often (and almost by definition) more complex than the reality it intends to capture. For instance, many technological solutions are used in the case of various innovations, and an innovation such as "big data analytics capabilities" (Benzidia et al., 2023) could either belong to technological innovation or process innovation. It depends at the same of the primary function and the degree of novelty of each type of innovation (in the particular case of big data analytics capabilities, because the primary function is about improving workflow and the technology is already existing, it would better fit the category of process innovation). Likewise, telemedicine (here placed as a service innovation) could also belong to technological innovation, but we considered that the service contribution was more important than the technological one. Even what appears to be the most aloof types of technology have more in common than what the graph could tell. For instance, technological innovation and frugal innovation, which could appear as the most distant forms of innovation (one high-tech and capital-intensive, the other low-cost and resource-conserving) can sometimes be complementary, as in the case of assisted diagnostics embedded in low-cost mobile kits. As some researchers suggest, this synergy allows health systems to "do more with less", while expanding reach and maintaining clinical quality (Bhatti & Ventresca, 2013). A second limitation is the positioning of the different types of innovations, which is made challenging by the diversity of solutions in each type of innovation. An educated guess was made in each case to rank them on both axis and to position them in the most sensible way. A third limitation is related to the static nature of the visualization, which cannot capture how innovations migrate across categories over time. As previously mentioned, novelty is situated, normative and contextual. Therefore, what begins as radical innovation in resource-constrained settings may become normalized service innovation when adopted by high-resource systems. Reversely, high-tech solutions may become frugal through local adaptation or contextual simplification. While the exact positioning can be discussed, the framework's primary value lies not in precise cartography but in revealing general patterns.

Now that we have positioned the different forms of innovation based on their degree of novelty and their impacts on the environment, one can question where the scientific literature stands to date. This is done in the next section (Fig. 4.4).

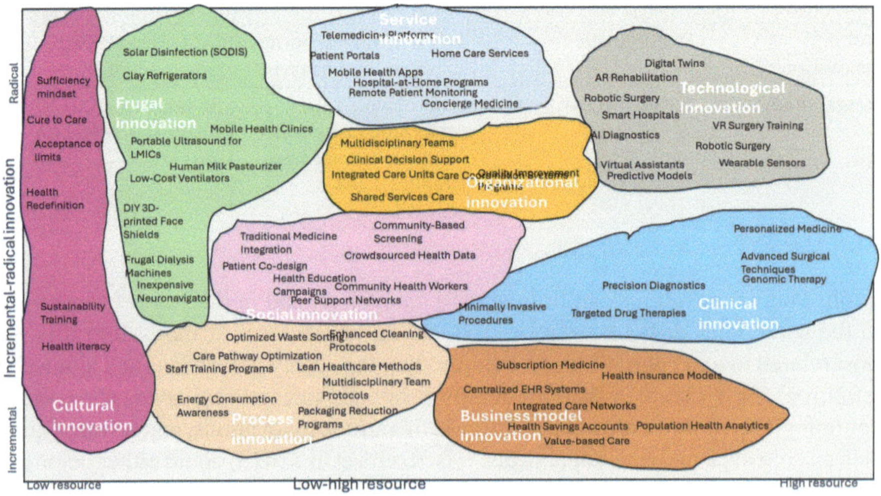

Fig. 4.4 Conceptual mapping of the nine forms of innovation

References

Aboueid, S., Beyene, M., & Nur, T. (2023). Barriers and enablers to implementing environmentally sustainable practices in healthcare: A scoping review and proposed roadmap. *Healthcare Management Forum, 36*(6), 405–413. https://doi.org/10.1177/08404704231183601

Adams, R., Tranfield, D., & Denyer, D. (2011). A taxonomy of innovation: Configurations of attributes in healthcare innovations. *International Journal of Innovation Management, 15*(02), 359–392. https://doi.org/10.1142/S1363919611003192

Adams, R., Tranfield, D. R., & Denyer, D. (2006). Innovation types: Configurations of attributes as a basis for innovation classification. *Advanced Institute of Management Research Paper*, (046). https://papers.ssrn.com/sol3/papers.cfm?abstract_id=1309554

Aggeri, F. (2023). *L'innovation, mais pour quoi faire?: Essai sur un mythe économique, social et managérial.* Seuil. https://books.google.fr/books?hl=fr&lr=&id=nSWzEAAAQBAJ&oi=fnd&pg=PA9&dq=L%27Innovation,+mais+pour+quoi+faire+%3F+Essai+sur+un+mythe+%C3%A9conomique,+social+et+manag%C3%A9rial&ots=1-6SjAOLj4&sig=MCU2Ve747Wy3UT4jz20_E_FNUeU

Ahmed, J. U., Gazi, M. A., Iqbal, R., Islam, Q. T., & Talukder, N. (2020). Value co-creation through social innovation in healthcare: A case of WE CARE Solar. *World Journal of Entrepreneurship, Management and Sustainable Development, 16*(4), 341–357.

Ahmed, F., Zhao, F., Faraz, N. A., & Qin, Y. J. (2021). How inclusive leadership paves way for psychological well-being of employees during trauma and crisis: A three-wave longitudinal mediation study. *Journal of Advanced Nursing, 77*(2), 819–831. https://doi.org/10.1111/jan.14637

Alami, H., Rivard, L., Lehoux, P., Ag Ahmed, M. A., Fortin, J.-P., & Fleet, R. (2023). Integrating environmental considerations in digital health technology assessment and procurement: Stakeholders' perspectives. *DIGITAL HEALTH, 9*, 20552076231219110. https://doi.org/10.1177/20552076231219113

Alter, N. (2010). *Les logiques de l'innovation: Approche pluridisciplinaire.* La découverte. https://books.google.fr/books?hl=fr&lr=&id=l6jBoLC8woQC&oi=fnd&pg=PA2&dq=alter+innovation&ots=d_xjuHx0VG&sig=WTmICUWY8IF1nuqRIHMKer0Uyv4

Arend, J., Tsang-Quinn, J., Levine, C., & Thomas, D. (2012). The patient-centered medical home: History, components, and review of the evidence. *Mount Sinai Journal of Medicine: A Journal of Translational and Personalized Medicine, 79*(4), 433–450. https://doi.org/10.1002/msj.21326

Arie, S. (2012). *US lags behind other countries in cutting numbers of preventable deaths.* British Medical Journal Publishing Group. https://www.bmj.com/content/345/bmj.e5937.short

Auer, R., Gencer, B., Räber, L., Klingenberg, R., Carballo, S., Carballo, D., Nanchen, D., Cornuz, J., Vader, J.-P., Vogt, P., Juni, P., Matter, C. M., Windecker, S., Lüscher, T. F., Mach, F., & Rodondi, N. (2014). Quality of care after acute coronary syndromes in a prospective cohort with reasons for non-prescription of recommended medications. *PloS one, 9*(3), e93147.

Barber, B., Rainham, D. G., Tyedmers, P., Vandertuin, T., Ritcey, G., & Christie, S. D. (2024). Taking action towards climate-resilient, low-carbon, health systems: Perspectives from Canadian health leaders and healthcare professionals. *Healthcare Management Forum, 37*(5), 395–400. https://doi.org/10.1177/08404704241252032

Barratt, A. L., Li, Y., Gooroovadoo, I., Todd, A., Dou, Y., McAlister, S., & Semsarian, C. (2023). Environmental impact of cardiovascular healthcare. *Open Heart, 10*(1), Article e002279. https://doi.org/10.1136/openhrt-2023-002279

Bateni, H., Carruthers, J., Mohan, R., & Pishva, S. (2024). Use of virtual reality in physical therapy as an intervention and diagnostic tool. *Rehabilitation Research and Practice, 2024*, 1–9. https://doi.org/10.1155/2024/1122286

Bauer, A., Hyánek, V., Figueroa, M. J., Sandford, S., Spalkova, D., Bardi, J., & Greiffenberg, C. (2016). *Social Innovation in health care.* https://research.cbs.dk/files/58551629/ITSSOIN_D5_5_Social_innovation_in_health_care.pdf

Benzidia, S., Bentahar, O., Husson, J., & Makaoui, N. (2024). Big data analytics capability in healthcare operations and supply chain management: The role of green process innovation. *Annals of Operations Research, 333*(2–3), 1077–1101. https://doi.org/10.1007/s10479-022-05157-6

Berger, M., Ehlers, J. P., & Nitsche, J. (2025). Aligning with the goals of the planetary health concept regarding ecological sustainability and digital health: Scoping review. *Journal of Medical Internet Research, 27*, Article e71795. https://doi.org/10.2196/71795

Berwick, D. M. (2003). *Disseminating Innovations in Health Care. Jama, 289*(15), 1969–1975.

Bhatti, Y. A., & Ventresca, M. (2013). How can 'frugal innovation'be conceptualized? *Available at SSRN 2203552.* https://papers.ssrn.com/sol3/papers.cfm?abstract_id=2203552

Biggi, G., & Giuliani, E. (2022). The noxious consequences of innovation: What do we know? In *The Dark Side of Innovation* (pp. 12–34). Routledge. https://www.taylorfrancis.com/chapters/edit/https://doi.org/10.4324/9781003259084-2/noxious-consequences-innovation-know-gianluca-biggi-elisa-giuliani

Bloomfield, P., Clutton-Brock, P., Pencheon, E., Magnusson, J., & Karpathakis, K. (2021). Artificial intelligence in the NHS: Climate and emissions. *The Journal of Climate Change and Health, 4*, Article 100056. https://doi.org/10.1016/j.joclim.2021.100056

Bounoure, F., Dupray, S., Wils, J., Taillemite, S., Brunn, M., Siefridt, C., Le Clech, N., Réveillon-Istin, M., Skiba, M., & Bouglé, C. (n.d.). Eco-prescription, a new major skill for healthcare professionals. *Annales Pharmaceutiques Francaises*, S0003–4509. Retrieved November 21, 2025, from https://pubmed.ncbi.nlm.nih.gov/41076239/

Bouwen, R., & Fry, R. (1991). Organizational innovation and learning: Four patterns of dialog between the dominant logic and the new logic. *International Studies of Management & Organization, 21*(4), 37–51. https://doi.org/10.1080/00208825.1991.11656566

Boyle, F., Hadgraft, R., Lindsay, E., & Ulseth, R. (2022). Innovating engineering education at Greenfield sites: Transferable insights from Doblin's Model of innovation. In *2022 IEEE frontiers in education conference (FIE)*, 1–8. https://ieeexplore.ieee.org/abstract/document/9962702/

Brown, H. (2007). Worsening security in Darfur could reverse health gains. *The Lancet, 369*(9562), 630–632.

Brulé, G., Boiko, P., Mezeray, T. M., Nadal, D., Vuilleumier, S., Senn, N., Fehr, J., Crivelli, L., Zinsstag, J., & Probst-Hensch, N. (2026). Can One Health help reduce the environmental impacts of the healthcare system in Switzerland? Insights from an interdisciplinary focus group. *Ethics, Medicine and Public Health, 34*, Article 101227.

Brulé, G., & Pichon, S. (2025). Promesses et défis de la télémédecine. In *Revue Hospitalière de France* (Vol.° 625, pp. 68–71).

Cambaza, E. (2023). The role of FinTech in sustainable healthcare development in sub-Saharan Africa: A narrative review. *FinTech, 2*(3), 444–460.

Castro-Arce, K., & Vanclay, F. (2020). Transformative social innovation for sustainable rural development: An analytical framework to assist community-based initiatives. *Journal of Rural Studies, 74*, 45–54.

Champendal, M., Lokaj, B., de Gevigney, V. D., Brulé, G., Zaghir, J., Boiko, P., Lovis, C., Müller, H., Schmid, J., & Ribeiro, R. T. (2025). Exploring environmental sustainability of artificial intelligence in radiology: A scoping review. *European Journal of Radiology*, 112558.

Charmillot, T., Chèvre, N., & Senn, N. (2025). Developing an ecotoxicological classification for frequently used drugs in primary care. *International Journal of Environmental Research and Public Health, 22*(2), 290.

Chavignon, A., Hingot, V., Orset, C., Vivien, D., & Couture, O. (2022). 3D transcranial ultrasound localization microscopy for discrimination between ischemic and hemorrhagic stroke in early phase. *Scientific Reports, 12*(1), 14607.

Chesbrough, H. (2010). Business model innovation: Opportunities and barriers. *Long Range Planning, 43*(2–3), 354–363.

Chopra, A. (2013). *The dark side of innovation.* Brigantine Media.

Cliff, B. Q., Avanceña, A. L. v., Hirth, R. A., & Lee, S.-Y. D. (2021). The impact of choosing wisely interventions on low-value medical services: A systematic review. *The Milbank Quarterly, 99*(4), 1024–1058. https://doi.org/10.1111/1468-0009.12531

Clinton, S. (2018). 18 a global network. *Promoting Biodiversity in Food Systems*, 317.

Collins, J. M., & Dempsey, M. K. (2019). Healthcare innovation methodology: Codifying the process of translating knowledge into better healthcare products, services, and procedures. *Current Opinion in Biomedical Engineering, 11*, 16–21.

Cosenz, F., Noto, G., Cavadi, G., Bivona, E., & Scirè, G. (2024). Pursuing sustainable performance in healthcare organizations: A sustainable business model perspective. *Journal of Health Organization and Management, 38*(5), 741–759.

Crema, M., & Verbano, C. (2017). Lean Management to support Choosing Wisely in healthcare: The first evidence from a systematic literature review. *International Journal for Quality in Health Care, 29*(7), 889–895.

Damanpour, F. (2017). Organizational innovation. In *Oxford research encyclopedia of business and management*. https://oxfordre.com/business/business/view/https://doi.org/10.1093/acrefore/9780190224851.001.0001/acrefore-9780190224851-e-19

Daniel, L. J., & Jenner, P. (2022). Another look at social innovation: From community-For community. *International Journal of Innovation Studies, 6*(2), 92–101.

Das, K. P., & Chandra, J. (2023). A survey on artificial intelligence for reducing the climate footprint in healthcare. *Energy Nexus, 9*, Article 100167.

Daughton, C. G., & Ruhoy, I. S. (2011). Green pharmacy and pharmEcovigilance: Prescribing and the planet. *Expert Review of Clinical Pharmacology, 4*(2), 211–232. https://doi.org/10.1586/ecp.11.6

Davenport, T. H. (1993). *Process innovation: Reengineering work through information technology*. Harvard Business Press. https://books.google.fr/books?hl=fr&lr=&id=kLlIOMGaKnsC&oi=fnd&pg=PR9&dq=davenport+1993+process+innovation&ots=_9kR-Gkuug&sig=rFEEsmCMR_airT9vEKoBSsRLssk

Davies, J. F., McAlister, S., Eckelman, M. J., McGain, F., Seglenieks, R., Gutman, E. N., Groome, J., Palipane, N., Latoff, K., & Nielsen, D. (2024). Environmental and financial impacts of perioperative paracetamol use: A multicentre international life-cycle assessment. *British Journal of Anaesthesia, 133*(6), 1439–1448.

de Ridder, E. F., Friedericy, H. J., van der Eijk, A. C., Dankelman, J., & Jansen, F. W. (2022). A new method to improve the environmental sustainability of the operating room: Healthcare sustainability mode and effect analysis (HSMEA). *Sustainability, 14*(21), 13957.

Deshpande, A. A., Mehta, S., & Kshirsagar, N. A. (2007). Hospital management of Mumbai train blast victims. *The Lancet, 369*(9562), 639–640.

Devis, L., Closset, M., Degosserie, J., Lessire, S., Modrie, P., Gruson, D., Favaloro, E. J., Lippi, G., Mullier, F., & Catry, E. (2025). Revisiting the environmental impact of inappropriate clinical laboratory testing: A comprehensive overview of sustainability, economic, and quality of care outcomes. *The Journal of Applied Laboratory Medicine, 10*(1), 113–129. https://doi.org/10.1093/jalm/jfae087

DiMaggio, P. (1997). *Culture and Cognition*.

Duan-Porter, W., Ullman, K., Majeski, B., Miake-Lye, I., Diem, S., & Wilt, T. J. (2022). Care coordination models and tools—systematic review and key informant interviews. *Journal of General Internal Medicine, 37*(6), 1367–1379. https://doi.org/10.1007/s11606-021-07158-w

Dziurski, P., & Wachowiak, P. (2021). Dark sides of innovation. In *Critical perspectives on innovation management* (pp. 101–114). Routledge. https://www.taylorfrancis.com/chapters/edit/https://doi.org/10.4324/9781003203841-8/dark-sides-innovation-patryk-dziurski-piotr-wachowiak

Ertelt, S.-M., & Carlborg, P. (2024). The dark sides of low-carbon innovations for net-zero transitions: A literature review and priorities for future research. *Sustainability: Science, Practice and Policy, 20*(1), 2335731. https://doi.org/10.1080/15487733.2024.2335731

Ertz, M., & Patrick, K. (2020). The future of sustainable healthcare: Extending product lifecycles. *Resources, Conservation and Recycling, 153*, Article 104589.

Fadda, J. (2020). Green healthcare system: Main features in supporting sustainability of healthcare system—a review. In A. Sayigh (Ed.), *Green buildings and renewable energy* (pp. 113–128). Springer International Publishing. https://doi.org/10.1007/978-3-030-30841-4_8

Field, M. J., & Lohr, K. N. (1990). Clinical practice guidelines. *Directions for a New Program, 1990*, 421.

Freeman, C., & Soete, L. (2009). Developing science, technology and innovation indicators: What we can learn from the past. *Research Policy, 38*(4), 583–589.

Gallouj, F., & Djellal, F. (2011). *The handbook of innovation and services: A multi-disciplinary perspective*. Edward Elgar Publishing. https://books.google.fr/books?hl=fr&lr=&id=r8dY6UJ979sC&oi=fnd&pg=PR1&dq=gallouj+service+innovation&ots=JPSYfVPAB7&sig=MDx4RfvNHOUadGrtuWrJkLp6OD0

Gallouj, F., & Weinstein, O. (1997). Innovation in services. *Research Policy, 26*(4–5), 537–556.

Garin, N., Zarate-Tamames, B., Lertxundi, U., da Silva, I. M., Orive, G., Crespo-Lessmann, A., & De la Rosa, D. (2025). The environmental impact of inhalers: A framework for sustainable prescription practices in Spain. *European Journal of Hospital Pharmacy*. https://ejhp.bmj.com/content/early/2025/01/09/ejhpharm-2024-004402.abstract

Gaudreau-Simard, M., Shetty, N., Silverstein, W. K., Luo, O. D., & Stoynova, V. (2025). Eight ways general internists can practice high-value, low-carbon care: The Canadian society of internal medicine's climate conscious choosing wisely Canada recommendations. *Journal of General Internal Medicine, 40*(7), 1609–1616.

Gault, F., Arundel, A., & Kraemer-Mbula, E. (2023). *Handbook of innovation indicators and measurement*. Edward Elgar Publishing. https://books.google.fr/books?hl=fr&lr=&id=cQXXEAAAQBAJ&oi=fnd&pg=PR1&dq=gault+handbook+&ots=P-jfdJXu_N&sig=CmHwvR-_jI5NEW93eHzmx9t7cZg

Gault, F. (2013). Innovation indicators and measurement: An overview. In *Handbook of Innovation Indicators and Measurement* (pp. 3–38).

Geels, F. W. (2002). Technological transitions as evolutionary reconfiguration processes: A multi-level perspective and a case-study. *Research Policy, 31*(8–9), 1257–1274.

Georgescu-Roegen, N. (2013). The Entropy Law and the Economic Process. *Harvard University Press*. https://doi.org/10.4159/harvard.9780674281653

Gerush, I., Khodorovskyy, V., Shchudrova, T., Korotun, O., & Bilous, T. (2024). *Overview of healthcare innovation and entrepreneurship*. https://dspace.bsmu.edu.ua/handle/123456789/25949

Ghaemi, S. N., & Goodwin, F. K. (2007). The ethics of clinical innovation in psychopharmacology: Challenging traditional bioethics. *Philosophy, Ethics, and Humanities in Medicine, 2*(1), 26. https://doi.org/10.1186/1747-5341-2-26

Giakoumakis, G., Politi, D., & Sidiras, D. (2021). Medical waste treatment technologies for energy, fuels, and materials production: A review. *Energies, 14*(23), 8065.

Gonzalez-Pizarro, P., Koch, S., Muret, J., Trinks, A., Brazzi, L., Reinoso-Barbero, F., Sebastian, J. D., & Struys, M. M. (2023). Environmental sustainability in the operating room: A worldwide survey among anaesthesiologists. *European Journal of Anaesthesiology and Intensive Care, 2*(4), e0025-e31.

Govindarajan, V., & Ramamurti, R. (2011). Reverse innovation, emerging markets, and global strategy. *Global Strategy Journal, 1*(3–4), 191–205. https://doi.org/10.1002/gsj.23

Haleem, A., Javaid, M., Singh, R. P., & Suman, R. (2021). Telemedicine for healthcare: Capabilities, features, barriers, and applications. *Sensors International, 2*, Article 100117.

Halford, W. K. (2020). Chapter 21 - Human families: Universalities, cultural variations, and family therapy practice implications. In W. K. Halford & F. van de Vijver (Eds.), *Cross-cultural family research and practice* (pp. 677–718). Academic Press. https://doi.org/10.1016/B978-0-12-815493-9.00021-1

Halpaap, B. M., Tucker, J. D., Mathanga, D., Juban, N., Awor, P., Saravia, N. G., Han, L., de Villiers, K., Kitamura, M., & Cuervo, L. G. (2020). Social innovation in global health: Sparking location action. *The Lancet Global Health, 8*(5), e633–e634.

Hammer, M., & Champy, J. (1993). *Business Process Reengineering. Nicholas Brealey, 444*(10), 730–755.

Hensher, M., & McGain, F. (2020). Health care sustainability metrics: building a safer, low-carbon health system: Commentary examines how to build a safer, low-carbon health system. *Health Affairs, 39*(12), 2080–2087. https://doi.org/10.1377/hlthaff.2020.01103

Herechuk, B., Gosse, C., & Woods, J. N. (2010). Achieving environmental excellence through a multidisciplinary grassroots movement. *Healthcare Management Forum, 23*(4), 144–149. https://doi.org/10.1016/j.hcmf.2010.08.008

Hersh, W. R., Totten, A. M., Eden, K. B., Devine, B., Gorman, P., Kassakian, S. Z., Woods, S. S., Daeges, M., Pappas, M., & McDonagh, M. S. (2015). Outcomes from health information exchange: Systematic review and future research needs. *JMIR Medical Informatics, 3*(4), Article e5215.

Herzlinger, R. E. (2006). Why innovation in health care is so hard. *Harvard Business Review, 84*(5), 58–66.

Hoxha, G., Simeli, I., Theocharis, D., Vasileiou, A., & Tsekouropoulos, G. (2024). Sustainable healthcare quality and job satisfaction through organizational culture: Approaches and outcomes. *Sustainability, 16*(9), 3603. https://doi.org/10.3390/su16093603

Jasanoff, S. (2004). *States of knowledge.* Taylor & Francis. https://api.taylorfrancis.com/content/books/mono/download?identifierName=doi&identifierValue=, https://doi.org/10.4324/9780203413845&type=googlepdf

Jeannerat, H., & Crevoisier, O. (2022). From competitiveness to territorial value: Transformative territorial innovation policies and anchoring milieus. *European Planning Studies, 30*(11), 2157–2177. https://doi.org/10.1080/09654313.2022.2042208

Jeannerat, H., Crevoisier, O., Brulé, G., & Suter, C. (2023). *L'apport des sciences humaines et sociales à l 'innovation en Suisse.* https://libra.unine.ch/handle/123456789/30481

Jimenez-Sanchez, G. (2015). Genomics innovation: Transforming healthcare, business, and the global economy. *Genome, 58*(12), 511–517. https://doi.org/10.1139/gen-2015-0121

Kar, S., Sanderson, H., Roy, K., Benfenati, E., & Leszczynski, J. (2022). Green chemistry in the synthesis of pharmaceuticals. *Chemical Reviews, 122*(3), 3637–3710. https://doi.org/10.1021/acs.chemrev.1c00631

Keil, M., Viere, T., Helms, K., & Rogowski, W. (2023). The impact of switching from single-use to reusable healthcare products: A transparency checklist and systematic review of life-cycle assessments. *European Journal of Public Health, 33*(1), 56–63.

Komenan, Y. (2025). Impact of green energy transition on healthcare infrastructure: A case study of MRI systems. *Journal of Scientific Research and Reports, 31*(3), 191–200.

van der Kooij, B. J. (2017). Search for a common ground in the fogs of innovation definitions. *Available at SSRN 3139486*. https://papers.ssrn.com/sol3/papers.cfm?abstract_id=3139486

Lahire, B. (2019). *Dans les plis singuliers du social-Individus, institutions, socialisations: Individus, institutions, socialisations.* La découverte. https://books.google.fr/books?hl=fr&lr=&id=_jqlDwAAQBAJ&oi=fnd&pg=PT8&dq=Dans+les+plis+singuliers+du+social&ots=pqu8Lreksl&sig=zK8Iftkq7jxIA67vQ4SgshanMAk

Lam, K., Gadi, N., Acharya, A., Beatty, J. W., Darzi, A., & Purkayastha, S. (2023). Interventions for sustainable surgery: A systematic review. *International Journal of Surgery, 109*(5), 1447–1458.

Lam, A. (2006). *Organizational innovation.* https://academic.oup.com/edited-volume/38667/chapter/335803708?searchresult=1&utm_source=TrendMD&utm_medium=cpc&utm_campaign=Oxford_Academic_Books_TrendMD_1

Leckie, B. (2020). Henry Mayhew, Urban Ecologist. *Victorian Literature and Culture, 48*(1), 219–241.

Leiden, A., Cerdas, F., Noriega, D., Beyerlein, J., & Herrmann, C. (2020). Life cycle assessment of a disposable and a reusable surgery instrument set for spinal fusion surgeries. *Resources, Conservation and Recycling, 156*, Article 104704.

Leswick, D. A., Kulanthaivelu, R., Jamil, H., Nguyen, C. L., Munir, O., Mirshahvalad, S. A., & Islam, O. (2025). Enhancing environmental sustainability in diagnostic radiology: Focus on CT, MRI, and nuclear medicine. Canadian Association of Radiologists Journal, 08465371251327143. https://doi.org/10.1177/08465371251327143

Lévi-Strauss, C. L. (1962). *Savage mind*. University of Chicago. https://web.mit.edu/allanmc/www/levistrauss.pdf

Li, Y., Cui, L., Wu, L., Lowry, P. B., Kumar, A., & Tan, K. H. (2024). Digitalization and network capability as enablers of business model innovation and sustainability performance: The moderating effect of environmental dynamism. *Journal of Information TechnologMarrauly, 39*(4), 687–715. https://doi.org/10.1177/02683962231219513

Lindskog, H. S., & Männer, J. B. (2019). Reduced climate impact by resource-efficient surgeries. *Lakartidningen, 116*, FHCU.

Lowden, L., & Henderson, C. (2025). Greening the lab: Creation of a national playbook on environmental sustainability in lab medicine. *Clinical Biochemistry*, 110963.

MacNeill, A. J., Rizan, C., & Sherman, J. D. (2024). Improving sustainability and mitigating the environmental impact of anaesthesia and surgery along the perioperative journey: A narrative review. *British Journal of Anaesthesia, 133*(6), 1397–1409. https://doi.org/10.1016/j.bja.2024.05.042

Manzini, E. (2014). Making things happen: Social innovation and design. *Design Issues, 30*(1), 57–66.

Mariano, S., & Casey, A. (2015). Is organizational innovation always a good thing? *Management Learning, 46*(5), 530–545. https://doi.org/10.1177/1350507615569429

Martuccelli, D. (2016). L'innovation, le nouvel imaginaire du changement. *Quaderni. Communication, Technologies, Pouvoir, 91*, 33–45.

Maughan, D. L., Patel, A., Parveen, T., Braithwaite, I., Cook, J., Lillywhite, R., & Cooke, M. (2016). Primary-care-based social prescribing for mental health: An analysis of financial and environmental sustainability. *Primary Health Care Research & Development, 17*(2), 114–121.

Mdleleni, L., & Velapi, L. (2022). Can Social Innovation advance the PMTCT programme? A South African reflection. *European Public & Social Innovation Review, 7*(1), 43–56.

Meadows, D. (2015). *Leverage points-places to intervene in a system*. https://mchwdc.unc.edu/wp-content/uploads/2022/04/Leverage-Points_Places-to-Intervene-in-a-System-Meadows.pdf

Meijer, A., & Thaens, M. (2021). The dark side of public innovation. *Public Performance & Management Review, 44*(1), 136–154. https://doi.org/10.1080/15309576.2020.1782954

Menachemi, N., Rahurkar, S., Harle, C. A., & Vest, J. R. (2018). The benefits of health information exchange: An updated systematic review. *Journal of the American Medical Informatics Association, 25*(9), 1259–1265.

Mikhailova, A. A., & Sharova, D. E. (2023). Artificial intelligence ethics code in healthcare. Sustainability of artificial intelligence systems: Why do we talk about their impact on the environment? *Digital Diagnostics, 4*(1S), 93–95.

Mishra, S., & Jain, K. (2025). Innovations in healthcare: A systematic literature review. *Journal of Business Research, 194*, Article 115364. https://doi.org/10.1016/j.jbusres.2025.115364

Moermond, C. T. A., Puhlmann, N., Brown, A. R., Owen, S. F., Ryan, J., Snape, J., Venhuis, B. J., & Kümmerer, K. (2022). GREENER pharmaceuticals for more sustainable healthcare. *Environmental Science & Technology Letters, 9*(9), 699–705. https://doi.org/10.1021/acs.estlett.2c00446

Molero, A., Calabrò, M., Vignes, M., Gouget, B., & Gruson, D. (2021). Sustainability in healthcare: Perspectives and reflections regarding laboratory medicine. *Annals of Laboratory Medicine, 41*(2), 139–144.

Morcillo Serra, C., Aroca Tanarro, A., Cummings, C. M., Jimenez Fuertes, A., & Tomás Martínez, J. F. (2022). Impact on the reduction of CO2 emissions due to the use of telemedicine. *Scientific Reports, 12*, 12507. https://doi.org/10.1038/s41598-022-16864-2

Moshawih, S., Wong, S. F., Woon, C. O., Lim, M. K., Ong, H. C., Goh, K. W., Gew, L. T., & Ming, L. C. (2025). Transforming healthcare sustainability: Circular economy approaches and stakeholder collaboration. *Sustainable Futures, 10*, Article 101199.

Moulaert, F., MacCallum, D., & Hillier, J. (2013a). Social innovation: Intuition, precept, concept, theory and practice. *The International Handbook on Social Innovation: Collective Action, Social Learning and Transdisciplinary Research, 13*, 13–24.

Moulaert, F., MacCallum, D., Mehmood, A., & Hamdouch, A. (2013b). General introduction: The return of social innovation as a scientific concept and a social practice. *The International Handbook on Social Innovation: Collective Action, Social Learning and Transdisciplinary Research, 1*, 1–6.

Ogburn, W. F. (1922). *Social change with respect to culture and original nature* (pp. 365).

Omachonu, V. K., & Einspruch, N. G. (2010). Innovation in healthcare delivery systems: A conceptual framework. *The Innovation Journal: THe Public Sector Innovation Journal, 15*(1), 1–20.

Osterwalder, A., & Pigneur, Y. (2010). *Business model generation: A handbook for visionaries, game changers, and challengers*. Wiley. https://books.google.fr/books?hl=fr&lr=&id=UzuTAwAAQBAJ&oi=fnd&pg=PP1&dq=osterwalder+business+model&ots=yZHRDiF91y&sig=ry0T40ZuP3JKvKhky7Ar-nPosbA

Osterwalder, A., & Pigneur, Y. (2013). *Business model generation: A handbook for visionaries, game changers, and challengers*. Wiley. https://books.google.fr/books?hl=fr&lr=&id=L3TnC7ZAWAsC&oi=fnd&pg=PP1&dq=Osterwalder++(2010)+business+mode&ots=gnhvnF02mG&sig=Sr69UnJv-IbigHzcUgq7kDro21M

Papadopoulou, A., Kumar, N. S., Vanhoestenberghe, A., & Francis, N. K. (2022). Environmental sustainability in robotic and laparoscopic surgery: Systematic review. *British Journal of Surgery, 109*(10), 921–932. https://doi.org/10.1093/bjs/znac191

Pereno, A., & Eriksson, D. (2020). A multi-stakeholder perspective on sustainable healthcare: From 2030 onwards. *Futures, 122*, Article 102605. https://doi.org/10.1016/j.futures.2020.102605

Pickard Strange, M., Booth, A., Akiki, M., Wieringa, S., & Shaw, S. E. (2023). The role of virtual consulting in developing environmentally sustainable health care: Systematic literature review. *Journal of Medical Internet Research, 25*, Article e44823.

Porter, M. E., & Teisberg, E. O. (2006). *Redefining health care: Creating value-based competition on results*. Harvard Business Press. https://books.google.fr/books?hl=fr&lr=&id=cse2LOAndNIC&oi=fnd&pg=PR10&dq=Porter+%26+Teisberg&ots=UrqGe7fYSp&sig=uYAmjMmUYLifQZGiAsLB_RiZrwY

Porter-O'Grady, T., & Malloch, K. (2010b). *Quantum Leadership:*. Jones & Bartlett Publishers. https://books.google.fr/books?hl=fr&lr=&id=_puPtgLYxJIC&oi=fnd&pg=PP1&dq=Porter-O%27Grady+%26+Malloch,+2010&ots=6GjFwe3a68&sig=KNGDAPpUhswum2Y-S7FA0UoykZI

Porter-O'Grady, T., & Malloch, K. (2010a). Innovation: Driving the green culture in healthcare. *Nursing Administration Quarterly, 34*(4), E1–E5.

Portes, A. (2021). Innovation as social change: An institutional analysis. *International Review of Sociology, 31*(3), 356–372. https://doi.org/10.1080/03906701.2021.2015983

Potera, C. (2012). Strategies for Greener Hospital operating rooms. *Environmental Health Perspectives, 120*(8), a. https://doi.org/10.1289/ehp.120-a306a

Pozzo, R., Filippetti, A., Paolucci, M., & Virgili, V. (2020). What does cultural innovation stand for? Dimensions, processes, outcomes of a new innovation category. *Science and Public Policy, 47*(3), 425–433. https://doi.org/10.1093/scipol/scaa023

Purohit, A., Smith, J., & Hibble, A. (2021). Does telemedicine reduce the carbon footprint of healthcare? *A Systematic Review. Future Healthcare Journal, 8*(1), Article e85.

Radjou, N., Prabhu, J., & Ahuja, S. (2012). *Jugaad innovation: Think frugal, be flexible, generate breakthrough growth*. Wiley. https://books.google.fr/books?hl=fr&lr=&id=6rFt9FwuV4gC&oi=fnd&pg=PR9&dq=radjou+frugal+innovation&ots=HWAQKOqUHM&sig=NsfNLVzYE_qiHjaK2BNyIhMLZok

Raghutla, C., & Chittedi, K. R. (2023). The effect of technological innovation and clean energy consumption on carbon neutrality in top clean energy-consuming countries: A panel estimation. *Energy Strategy Reviews, 47*, Article 101091.

Ramdorai, A., & Herstatt, C. (2015). Frugal innovation in healthcare: How targeting low-income markets leads to disruptive innovation. *Springer International Publishing*. https://doi.org/10.1007/978-3-319-16336-9

Ravindrane, R., & Patel, J. (2022). Infrastructure: The environmental impacts of telemedicine in place of face-to-face patient care: A systematic review. *Future Healthcare Journal, 9*(1), 28–33.

Rogers, E. M. (1995). Lessons for guidelines from the diffusion of innovations. *The Joint Commission Journal on Quality Improvement, 21*(7), 324–328.

Rogers, E. M., Singhal, A., & Quinlan, M. M. (2014). Diffusion of innovations. In *An integrated approach to communication theory and research* (pp. 432–448). Routledge. https://www.taylorfrancis.com/chapters/edit/https://doi.org/10.4324/9780203887011-36/diffusion-innovations-everett-rogers-arvind-singhal-margaret-quinlan

Rønn, C., Wieland, A., Lehrer, C., Márton, A., LaRoche, J., Specker, A., Leroy, P., & Fürstenau, D. (2023). Circular business model for digital health solutions: Protocol for a scoping review. *JMIR Research Protocols, 12*(1), Article e47874.

Rosenthal, M. B., Friedberg, M. W., Singer, S. J., Eastman, D., Li, Z., & Schneider, E. C. (2013). Effect of a multipayer patient-centered medical home on health care utilization and quality: The Rhode Island chronic care sustainability initiative pilot program. *JAMA Internal Medicine, 173*(20), 1907–1913.

Samuel, G., & Lucassen, A. M. (2023). The environmental impact of data-driven precision medicine initiatives. *Cambridge Prisms: Precision Medicine, 1*, Article e1.

Schein, E. H. (2010). *Organizational culture and leadership* (Vol. 2). Wiley. https://books.google.fr/books?hl=fr&lr=&id=DlGhlT34jCUC&oi=fnd&pg=PR9&dq=schein+culture&ots=-ft_3pUkCU&sig=Iwf3ladvVUOVjjCLCSYrVFNIS0A

Schumpeter, J. (1942). *Creative destruction*. https://books.google.fr/books?hl=fr&lr=&id=NRxUEAAAQBAJ&oi=fnd&pg=PA421&dq=schumpeter+1942&ots=ay_B1iNWB2&sig=VwJpE0eyDHpegInc6oimZ0DSTmc

Seifert, C., Koep, L., Wolf, P., & Guenther, E. (2021). Life cycle assessment as decision support tool for environmental management in hospitals: A literature review. *Health Care Management Review, 46*(1), 12–24.

Shaner-McRae, H., & Jas, V. (2007). Environmentally safe health care agencies: Nursing's responsibility, Nightingale's Legacy. *Online Journal of Issues in Nursing, 12*(2), N_A.

Sinaiko, A. D., Landrum, M. B., Meyers, D. J., Alidina, S., Maeng, D. D., Friedberg, M. W., Kern, L. M., Edwards, A. M., Flieger, S. P., Houck, P. R., Peele, P., Reid, R. J., McGraves-Lloyd, K., Finison, K., & Rosenthal, M. B. (2017). Synthesis of research on patient-centered medical homes brings systematic differences into relief. *Health Affairs, 36*(3), 500–508. https://doi.org/10.1377/hlthaff.2016.1235

Sittig, D. F., Sherman, J. D., Eckelman, M. J., Draper, A., & Singh, H. (2022). I-CLIMATE: A "clinical climate informatics" action framework to reduce environmental pollution from healthcare. *Journal of the American Medical Informatics Association, 29*(12), 2153–2160. https://doi.org/10.1093/jamia/ocac137

Sounderajah, V., Patel, V., Varatharajan, L., Harling, L., Normahani, P., Symons, J., Barlow, J., Darzi, A., & Ashrafian, H. (2021). Are disruptive innovations recognised in the healthcare literature? A systematic review. *BMJ Innovations, 7*(1). https://innovations.bmj.com/content/7/1/208.abstract

Sullivan, G. A., Petit, H. J., Reiter, A. J., Westrick, J. C., Hu, A., Dunn, J. B., Gulack, B. C., Shah, A. N., Dsida, R., & Raval, M. V. (2023). Environmental impact and cost savings of operating room quality improvement initiatives: A scoping review. *Journal of the American College of Surgeons, 236*(2), 411–423.

Sveiby, K.-E. (2017). Unattended consequences of innovation. In *Critical studies of innovation* (pp. 137–156). Edward Elgar Publishing. https://www.elgaronline.com/edcollchap/edcoll/9781785366963/9781785366963.00016.xml

Swałek, A., & Steinerowska-Streb, I. (2023). Greening healthcare delivery: A path to sustainable development in Silesian Public Hospitals. *Scientific Papers of Silesian University of Technology. Organization & Management/Zeszyty Naukowe Politechniki Slaskiej. Seria Organizacji i Zarzadzanie*, (189). https://managementpapers.polsl.pl/wp-content/uploads/2024/02/189-Swa%C5%82ek-Steinerowska-Streb.pdf

Tan, K., & Zhang, J. (2025). Uncovering the carbon footprint of minimally invasive axillary osmidrosis surgery in China through life cycle assessment. *Scientific Reports, 15*(1), 21515. https://doi.org/10.1038/s41598-025-09293-4

Tanner, E. (1996). Why things bite back. *Technology and the Revenge of Unintended.*

Thiel, C. L., Mehta, N., Sejo, C. S., Qureshi, L., Moyer, M., Valentino, V., & Saleh, J. (2023). Telemedicine and the environment: Life cycle environmental emissions from in-person and virtual clinic visits. *NPJ Digital Medicine, 6*(1), 87.

Tiase, V. L., Hull, W., McFarland, M. M., Sward, K. A., Del Fiol, G., Staes, C., Weir, C., & Cummins, M. R. (2020). Patient-generated health data and electronic health record integration: A scoping review. *JAMIA Open, 3*(4), 619–627.

Tidd, J., & Bessant, J. R. (2014). *Strategic innovation management*. Wiley. https://books.google.fr/books?hl=fr&lr=&id=V2QJEQAAQBAJ&oi=fnd&pg=PR1&dq=tidd+bessant+2009&ots=IuRF6cqZUt&sig=DHmrBF1JInf5HG6_OIBMa5bH0ow

Tjokro, K. J., Barbarossa, V., Cucurachi, S., Rwei, A., & Lian, J. (2025). Assessing the environmental impacts of microfluidic devices for glucose detection. *ACS Sustainable Chemistry & Engineering, 13*(25), 9500–9509. https://doi.org/10.1021/acssuschemeng.5c01511

Tokgöz, P., Stampa, S., Wähnert, D., Vordemvenne, T., & Dockweiler, C. (2022). Virtual reality in the rehabilitation of patients with injuries and diseases of upper extremities. *Healthcare, 10*(6), 1124. https://www.mdpi.com/2227-9032/10/6/1124

Townend, W. K., & Cheeseman, C. R. (2005). Guidelines for the evaluation and assessment of the sustainable use of resources and of wastes management at healthcare facilities. *Waste Management & Research: THe Journal for a Sustainable Circular Economy, 23*(5), 398–408. https://doi.org/10.1177/0734242X05057764

Ulhøi, J. P., & Ulhøi, B. P. (2009). Beyond climate focus and disciplinary myopia. The roles and responsibilities of hospitals and healthcare professionals. *International Journal of Environmental Research and Public Health, 6*(3), 1204–1214.

Upadhyay, U., Gradisek, A., Iqbal, U., Dhar, E., Li, Y.-C., & Syed-Abdul, S. (2023). Call for the responsible artificial intelligence in the healthcare. *BMJ Health & Care Informatics, 30*(1), Article e100920. https://doi.org/10.1136/bmjhci-2023-100920

Van de Ven, A. H., Polley, D. E., Garud, R., & Venkataraman, S. (1999). Building an infrastructure for the innovation journey. *The Innovation Journey, 149*, 180.

Wang, W., Zhang, J., Mitchell, R., Nicholas, S., Maitland, E., Lu, J., & Liu, X. (2025). Psychological safety and primary care physicians' well-being, work conditions and guideline adherence behavior: A cross-sectional study in China. *Global Health Action, 18*(1), 2484096. https://doi.org/10.1080/16549716.2025.2484096

Wiersma, M., Kerridge, I., & Lipworth, W. (2025). A Multidisciplinary model for the Governance of Clinical innovation: Insights from a qualitative study of Australian Doctors. *Evaluation & the Health Professions*, 01632787251324662. https://doi.org/10.1177/01632787251324662

Willie, M. M. (2024). Service innovation theory and its application in healthcare. *Journal of Healthcare in Developing Countries (JHCDC), 4*(2), 57–65.

Wolf, R. M., Abramoff, M. D., Channa, R., Tava, C., Clarida, W., & Lehmann, H. P. (2022). Potential reduction in healthcare carbon footprint by autonomous artificial intelligence. *NPJ Digital Medicine, 5*(1), 62.

Wormer, B. A., Augenstein, V. A., Carpenter, C. L., Burton, P. V., Yokeley, W. T., Prabhu, A. S., Harris, B., Norton, S., Klima, D., Lincourt, A. E., & Heniford, B. T. (2013). The green operating room: simple changes to reduce cost and our carbon footprint. *The American Surgeon, 79*(7), 666–671.

Chapter 5
A Critical Perspective of Innovation in the Healthcare Sector

Abstract The present chapter critically examines the relative weight of each of the nine forms of innovation as per its number of publications in the scientific literature. The technical form of innovation dominates the literature whereas other forms of innovation such as organizational or frugal innovation are misrepresented. The literature further shows a strong focus on western, medical innovation and male innovation. An analysis of the scientific imaginaries through bibliometric analysis reveals a preference of the cure over the care, a "more is better" type of thinking and an importance of the present over the future.

Keywords High-tech · low-tech · imaginaries · barriers · levers

Arguably, innovations have often been reduced to innovators, forgetting the ecosystems that enabled them, the public aids that made them possible in the first place (Berkun, 2010). Still, it is impossible to talk about innovation without talking about innovators. As we shall see, innovations in the healthcare sector are dominated by a western, masculine, and medical imaginaries. Part of this reason is that, as demonstrated by Lehoux et al. (2016) and Harris et al. (2018), innovation studies systematically privilege formal, documented, institution-backed initiatives while excluding informal, practice-based, and community-generated solutions. For instance, grassroots innovations are frequently invisible in standard metrics of innovation because they are undocumented, informal, or disqualified because they do not fit dominant paradigms of value, novelty, or patentability. As Harris et al. (2018) argue, "what you find depends on where you look".

G. Brulé, *Reducing the Environmental Impact of Healthcare Systems*, Sustainable Business Development, https://doi.org/10.1007/978-3-032-34889-0_5

What Innovations?

Recently, we have questioned for whom the innovation in healthcare was (Baras et al., 2026). Questioning whether innovation was targeting clinical, social, economic, or environmental benefits, this looks for whom innovation is directed in the healthcare sector. As illustrated in Table 5.1, the distribution reveals that healthcare innovation discourse unsurprisingly prioritizes clinical outcomes, while environmental considerations receive significantly less attention.

Innovation at What Stage

An alternative approach to analyzing innovation in the healthcare sector is to look at what stage of the 5R (Refuse, Reduce, Reuse, Recycle, and Rethink) framework the innovation belongs (see Table 5.2).

This distribution reveals healthcare "downstream tropism" as far as sustainability is concerned, with a focus on "Recycle". The modest presence of "Refuse" and "Rethink" approaches suggests that an interest is present, but their secondary status shows that transformative approaches come after reformist approaches. As for the indicators, the downstream solutioning dominates while the upstream thinking is underrepresented.

Beyond Techno-productive Innovation

Observing what innovation is favored through scientific publications provides an idea of where the focus is in this grammar of innovations. This is illustrated in Table 5.3.

The results presented in the table above show that the focus of innovation in sustainable healthcare leans on the technoproductive side. Sustainability is seen as a

Table 5.1 main reasons for environment-saving innovations

Category	Article count
Patient/Clinical	1150
Social	524
Economic	348
Environmental	227

Source Pubmed. Dates: all. See details in Appendix A

Table 5.2 strategy according to the 5R framework

Strategy	Article count
Refuse	31
Reduce	24
Reuse	52
Rethink	31
Recycle	77

Source Pubmed. Dates: all. See details in Appendix A

Table 5.3 Number of publications per form of innovation

Innovation main category	Innovation subtype	Number of publications
Technoproductive	Technological	197
Technoproductive	Service	31
Technoproductive	Clinical	50
Socio-organizational	Process	17
Socio-organizational	Organizational	11
Socio-organizational	Business model	19
Socio-organizational	Social	17
Paradigmatic	Frugal	13
Paradigmatic	Cultural	21

Source Pubmed. Dates: all. See details in Appendix A

problem to fix through more tools and devices rather than a preoccupation with the social, organizational, cultural or the lean side. This isn't so surprising. As shown by Harmut Rosa (2003), innovation is co-substantial with acceleration. This is however concerning in many ways. Over the past two decades, healthcare innovation has been increasingly dominated by the language of digital transformation, artificial intelligence, genomics, and personalized medicine. These narratives are powerful because they speak to a deep collective desire for control, mastery, and infinite progress. They promise faster diagnostics, more tailored therapies, and enhanced health system efficiency. Yet these technological trajectories are not without ecological cost. High-tech care infrastructures require high-density energy, intensive computation, and globally distributed supply chains. The environmental burden of these technologies is far from magical. AI systems, particularly large models used for diagnostics, natural language processing, and treatment prediction, rely on data centers with massive energy demands, at a moment where the sector tries to cut its energy needs. Personalized medicine depends on short-lifecycle diagnostic devices and biologics with complex cold chains, often yielding significant emissions and material waste. The global push toward digitization also generates a rising wave of electronic waste, obsolescence, and resource extraction tied to rare metals. As highlighted by Udegbe et al. (2024), the data infrastructures underlying AI in healthcare, from wearables to remote monitoring, often depend on continuous energy input and generate invisible forms of digital pollution through data storage, transmission, and algorithmic processing. *Beyond patents and investment in R&D* There are many metrics used to measure innovation. Most of the work on indicators of innovation were done by Fred Gault, who has extensively analyzed how innovation was measured (Gault, 2013). In a previous work, we have identified what academic disciplines were related to innovation, in particular in the Swiss context (Jeannerat et al., 2023). To date, the room left to sustainability in innovation metrics has hardly been questioned. If we take a look at some of the main indicators used to measure innovation, it is possible to see that the environment is not absent, but that most metrics do not have an explicit environmental dimension. This is even more true if one looks at it closer, since, from the perspective of the main indicators (number of patents, number of publications, investment in R&D), which all have a blind eye on environmental impacts. This is also true when looking at indexes of innovation such as the Global Innovation Index that dedicate only a small part to environmental matters.

Innovation by Whom?

Beyond Colonial Innovation

The fact that innovation is used as a way for countries to bring their domination on others is not new. During the European conquest of New World and the following slavery, the idea of novelty was used as a differentiator between the civilized West and populations that were "closer to Nature" (Boumediene, 2016; Guien, 2025). This is also visible in everyday literature. In order to keep the productive species, Robinson Crusoe eliminates the natives and keeps Friday under custody. Where are the official innovators trying to reduce the environmental impacts of the healthcare sector from? The publications stem from institutions (universities, hospitals, clinics...) from OECD countries, with the UK (37.4%) and US (27.3%) alone account for nearly two-thirds of healthcare sustainability innovation publications, despite representing less than 5% of global population. On the other side of the spectrum, countries representing approximately 75% of global population contribute only 4.3% of healthcare sustainability innovation research. The geographic distribution shown in Table 5.4 reveals several blind spots in healthcare sustainability as the Global North is the origin of the lion's share of the publications. This means that the architecture of knowledge carries blind spots and that, as for other fields (AI, soft power), the voice of the Global South is virtually unheard.

Table 5.4 countries of origin of publications on the environmental sustainability sector

Country/region	Publications	% of Total	Publications per 100 M population
England	70	37.4%	125.0
United States	51	27.3%	15.4
Netherlands	18	9.6%	105.9
Switzerland	12	6.4%	133.3
Germany	7	3.7%	8.4
France	5	2.7%	7.4
Australia	2	1.1%	7.7
Canada	2	1.1%	5.3
Global South Total	8	4.3%	0.1
Other High-Income	12	6.4%	3.0

Source Pubmed. Dates: all. See details in Appendix A

The crual irony in the case of environmental health is that, as we have seen through frugal innovation, the Global South might detain missing pieces to reduce the environmental impact of the healthcare system in the Global North. As a matter of fact, countries like India have been leaders in frugal innovation or "jugaad" innovation (which means "manage" in Hindhi). This raises at least two issues. First, innovation solutions are developed primarily by and for high-resource settings, potentially missing more sustainable approaches developed under resource constraints. High-tech solutions from well-resourced environments may prove inappropriate for resource-constrained settings where most healthcare is delivered. Second, this is a lack of visibility of solutions which might prove particularly robust, including for the Global North which is increasingly depending on electricity and technological solutions. While this might work most of the time, it also raises problems when electricity installations face issues as seen in April 2025 in Spain/Portugal when a power cut during which every hospital had trouble operating.

Beyond Medical Innovation

In order to further sktech the profile of the innovator, we must turn toward what professions are typically considered as innovators. The analysis of which healthcare professions are represented in sustainability innovation literature reveals strong hierarchies that may fundamentally bias the types of solutions that emerge as shown in Table 5.5.

The publications by medical doctors are ahead of all other professions combined. This shows a clear pattern of the medicalization of innovation, i.e., the edge medical doctors have on innovation in the healthcare sector. This can be explained by higher cultural capital and prestige (Çitaku et al., 2012; Plochg & Hamer, 2012; Van Wijngaarden et al., 2012) in a context where the medicalization of care delivery has led to a dominant figure defined by technical precision, scientific rationality, and adherence to standardized protocols. This was already present in the Flexner Report (1910). Environmental consciousness, when it appears at all, is peripheral. Reversely, the

Table 5.5 professions mentioned in the publications on initiatives to reduce environmental impacts in the healthcare sector

Title	Results (PubMed)	Percentage %	Results (OpenAlex)	Percentage %
Medical doctors	195	55.9	6811	39.1
Nurses	98	28.1	4711	27.1
Pharmacists	17	4.9	2061	11.8
Physiotherapists	9	2.6	1106	6.4
Midwives	8	2.3	773	4.4
Radiological imaging	6	1.7	79	0.5
Nutritionists	16	4.6	1859	10.7
Total	349	100.0	17,400	100.0

Source Pubmed / OpenAlex. Dates: all. See details in Appendix A

underrepresentation of other professions translates in missed opportunities in terms of innovation. Although innovations are often claimed by professions with the most cultural capital, many innovations are done on the ground by the forefront workers, as already claimed by Adam Smith in *The Wealth of Nations*:

> All the improvements in machinery, however, have by no means been the inventions of those who had occasion to use the machines. Many improvements have been made by the ingenuity of the makers of the machines, when to make them became the business of a peculiar trade; and some by that of those who are called philosophers or men of speculation, whose trade it is not to do anything, but to observe everything; and who, upon that account, are often capable of combining together the powers of the most distant and dissimilar objects. In the progress of society, philosophy or speculation becomes, like every other employment, the principal or sole trade and occupation of a particular class of citizens. Like every other employment too, it is subdivided into a great number of different branches, each of which affords occupation to a peculiar tribe or class of philosophers; and this subdivision of employment in philosophy, as well as in every other business, improves dexterity, and saves time. Each individual becomes more expert in his own peculiar branch, more work is done upon the whole, and the quantity of science is considerably increased by it.

Craftsmen and blue-collar workers in the face of difficulties have often invented solutions to bypass them. They have often been invisibilized and the innovations were claimed by the management or the factories, to which the inventions belong. The construction of professional identity is not only positive but negative, i.e., against other professions. Medical professionals distinguish themselves from "alternative" practitioners, social workers, or environmental advocates partly by emphasizing their commitment to scientific rigor, technological mastery, and evidence-based practice. Since sustainability is often based on principles of precaution and not always on hard data, advocating for sustainability is a risk of trespassing the boundaries of legitimate medical expertise and be considered as "less serious".

Beyond Masculine Innovation

The question of who conducts innovation from a gender perspective has received attention in various settings (Mendonca & Reis, 2020; Schøtt & Cheraghi, 2015), less so in healthcare contexts despite exceptions (Cheon et al., 2022). To explore potential gendered differences, we analyzed the first names of lead authors in a recent corpus of 2025 publications retrieved from PubMed. Gender inference was initially performed using the Genderize API based on the first name of the first author. For names with ambiguous, rare, or culturally unfamiliar profiles, or for which the probability was below a confidence threshold (typically <0.70), we conducted manual verification through institutional affiliations and visual identification via institutional websites or academic profiles. As illustrated in Table 5.6, the gendered segmentation is remarkable. Among publications centered on technological innovation, we found that only 25% of first authors were women, whereas in the social innovation corpus, 70% of first authors were women. These results suggest a gendered orientation in the way innovation types within the healthcare literature are structured or divided. Men appear more frequently in domains linked to high-tech and digital tools, while women more often author work related to social and organizational innovation. Although not definitive, this observation resonates with previous findings on gendered divisions of

Table 5.6 Sex of the first authors in publications on initiatives to reduce the environmental impacts in the healthcare sector (period: first half of 2025)

Innovation type	Sample size	Women first authors	Men first authors	Pattern analysis
Technological Innovation	91	23 (25%)	68 (75%)	Strong male dominance in tech-focused innovation
Social innovation	64	45 (70%)	19 (30%)	Strong female leadership in social/organizational innovation

Source Pubmed. Dates: first half of 2025. See details in Appendix A

labor. This is also another way sustainability and gender equality resonate(Merchant, 2010).

These results suggest possible gendered orientations in innovation types within healthcare literature that have been observed elsewhere (Ragasa, 2012; Zhou & Xu, 2007). Men predominate in technological innovation domains linked to high-tech and digital tools, artificial intelligence, and medical devices, while women dominate as far as social innovations are concerned such as community-based interventions, behavioral change approaches, and people-centered design. The valorization of high-tech interventions over preventive or ecological approaches reflects deeply gendered divisions about what constitutes legitimate medical knowledge and practice.

What Imaginaries

After questioning the tools (*technè [τέχνη]*), the procedures, and the representations of the innovators, we must now more fundamentally question the imaginaries upon which our healthcare systems rely. Following Foucault's archaeology, we must examine how certain practices become so entranched in institutional discourse that they come to appear natural rather than historically constructed.

When Technè Means Techno

When Alter says "innovation requires a touch of magical thinking", it seems that, since a few decades, the genius takes the form of a modern, technological equipment. The expertise in a given field is what the Greeks called *technè*. From the Ancient Greece to the Middle Ages, technè echoed an art, local, unique form of know-how. Technè was then unique, micro and situated. The Industrial Revolution changed the imaginary and associated technè to machinery, reproduction and industrial. Technè then became reproducible, macro and standardized. The field of health was later conditioned by that shift with the Pasteurian revolution which equated health progress to hygiene, cleanliness, sanitization. In the twentieth century, hospitals gradually became machines for diagnosis and treatment with medical instruments (thermometers, stethoscopes, sphygmomanometers) and laboratory diagnostics (urinalysis, blood counts), emphasizing objectivity and spatial control (Foucault, 2002). This was deeply anchored by several waves such as the rise of biomedicine, the technodevelopment of post-Second World War, the digitalization and the COVID-19 effect. Power dynamics reinforce that tendency by aligning symbolic capital and prestige (in general physicians) to mastery of complex technologies over behavioral (nurses, community health professionals, psychologists, social workers…) (Gaspar et al., 2025). This is still the case today. A 2019 Euro-BioImaging survey of 117 infrastructure users and 106 providers across Europe revealed that the most requested "innovative" technologies had high-intensity. MRI variants came first, followed by advanced computational imaging techniques (light-sheet microscopy, ultra-high-resolution microscopy, and positron emission tomography). Technologies coming at the top of the ladder demand substantial capital investment, energy consumption, and specialized infrastructure (Euro-BioImaging, 2019).

Healthcare's axiological structure can be understood around opposing poles of purity and impurity. In healthcare, high-tech innovations, which appear as objective, scientific, and universal, occupy the "pure" pole while other forms of innovation such as low-tech, social, or behavioral interventions seem contextual, subjective, and primitive and are relegated to the "impure" pole (Bourdieu, 1988). This purification process generates the powerful illusion that technology transcends the messy social realities of healthcare delivery, while frugal approaches, which acknowledge social and economic constraints, appear "compromised" or insufficiently medical (Fig. 5.1).

Plastic Is Fantastic

When healthcare professionals are asked about the main impacts of their sector, wastes, and plastics in particular, often comc first. In fact, the amount of plastic wastes generated in HC settings is preoccupying. A German surgical hospital study revealed the use of 531 grams of polymers (incl. 45% of polypropylene and 25% of

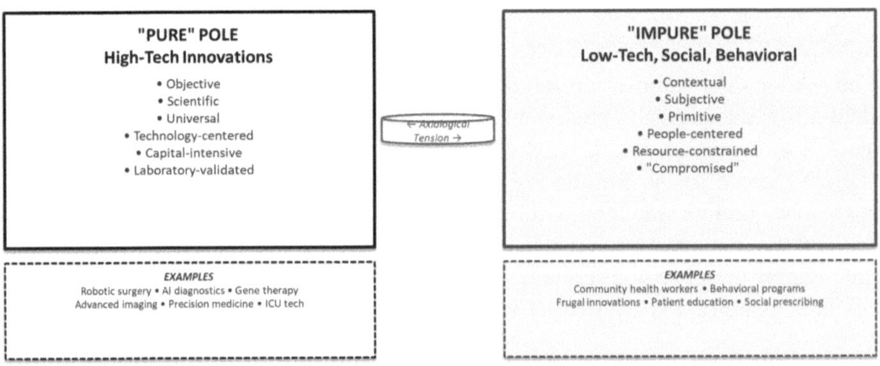

Fig. 5.1 Conceptual purification of forms of innovation

latex) consumed per patient per day, representing 86% of medical consumables, with personal protective equipment and incontinence products constituting the largest categories (Ivanović et al., 2022). This is not limited to high-income countries as an Indian study shows that 18% of biomedical waste and 13% of general waste consisted of plastic material (Dutt Bhardwaj et al., 2023). Plastic is ubiquitous in all phases of healthcare delivery (preventive, diagnostic, therapeutic, prosthetic, and palliative care phases) (Sivaram et al., 2021). Although we have here mostly focused on environmental impacts, there are now concerns that chemicals may leach from plastic additives, hereby affecting vulnerable patient population (Ramos et al., 2023). As we have mentioned earlier in this book, this is not where the most impacts are at least when looking at the most common measure of the carbon footprint, nor is it the case with the complementary measure explored in this book of material footprint but it impacts the imaginaries and the feelings of many healthcare workers. It is also the most direct resource these workers have their disposal, see and touch on a daily basis. Many express on the ground feeling sick by throwing away so much.[1] In the healthcare culture, the "disposable logic" emerged as a discursive formation that emerged in the 1970s and 1980s. It is not an absolute necessity, but a given narrative present in western societies (and since then in others) since about half a century.

Cure vs *Care*

Medicalization describes a process where more and more aspects of human existence, human behavior, and the human body are reframed as medical issues and where the professional power of medicine expands over wider spheres of life (Foucault, 2002, p. 135). The role of the modern hospital is to cure, fix the body and the mind. As we have seen, the physicians and the administrators are the conductors of that theater. The relative positions of healthcare professionals can be understood in relation to their specific forms of capital within the medical field (Bourdieu & Wacquant, 1992; Canguilhem, 1966). The more specialized and the more technicized, the higher the prestige; the less specialized and the less technicized, the lower the position on the prestige ladder. Also, nurses follow that same order, with the most technical and the most urgent dominating the prestige ladder whereas the nurses busy with community, prevention, and social work occupy the bottom of the ladder (Longchamp et al., 2015).

The shift that happened to the healthcare sector, which is, the shift from care to cure is the same that happened in other sectors. In the same way GDP became a proxy for quality of life, the good cure became a proxy for the good care. Whereas this approximation (good cure = good care) might have been true in the middle of the twentieth century, it seems to lose its legitimacy with time. In the same way economic growth was a decent proxy for good life in the middle of the twentieth century, curing might have been a decent proxy for good care in the mid-twentieth century. However, in both cases, the benefits of that simplification have gradually saturated, and the side effects have become increasingly clear. The fact that an indicator can serve as a proxy at a given moment and might lose its capacity over time is a form of Goodhart's law,

---

[1] Heard many times in HC settings in France, Switzerland, and Luxembourg.

which that when a measure becomes a target, it ceases to be a good measure. This indicator reification shows how much the institutionalization of the norms and values can work for a time, but rarely *ad vitaernam.* Most of the time, instead of cohabiting, the logics of care and cure confront. As Apesoa-Varano (2007) shows in her ethnography of nursing education, professional socialization often revolves around embodying dual ideals: scientific authority and emotional care. These can be complementary but are frequently in tension. This cure-as-a-care form of reduction, whereby individual bodies are "restored" to a presumed state of normalcy overlooks other forms of care. In particular, preventive, relational, and ecological dimensions are overshadowed of care, as well as unpaid and informal practices of support that sustain life beyond the clinic, such as community support, environmental protection and restoration, which have long been emphasized in feminist and postcolonial literature. Yet, in dominant healthcare imaginaries, these dimensions are often subordinated to abstract metrics and standardized protocols.

In that sense, feminist political ecologists define planetary care as a shift from control to coexistence, from mastery to response-ability (Puig de La Bellacasa, 2013). Winders & Smith (2019) remind us that care cannot be disentangled from political economy. Under capitalism, both ecosystems and caregiving labor are extracted and undervalued (Merchant, 2014). Health is then treated as a market good rather than a shared responsibility for supporting community well-being. The development of planetary care values also requires attention to other knowledge systems. A "two-eyed" perspective with western and indigenous considerations (Illes et al., 2025) can embody planetary care principles through integration of human health with ecological well-being, their emphasis on relationship and reciprocity, and their attention to long-term consequences across generations.

More Is Better vs *Good Enough*

The current mantra of the healthcare setting seems to be "more is better". Bodies and minds should be fixed at any cost for as long as possible no matter what. As a significant share of the healthcare costs and thus a high part of the environmental impacts occurs within the last year of life (Aldridge & Kelley, 2015), professional association have started to question this mantra of maintaining life and extending life in any situation. The Swiss association of intensive medicine has mentioned in its top 5 for smarter medicine to not pursue care with people with severe risks of dying without discussing the therapeutic goals with the patients or the represent of the patient.[2] McNamara (2004) documents how the theoretical ideal of "good death" has been replaced by a pragmatic notion of "good enough death". The notion of "good enough" could save a lot of resources with virtually no cost in terms of quality of care (Brulé et al., 2026). Interviewing healthcare workers during the COVID-19 pandemic, Harrison et al. (2023) distinguish the "familiar", "good enough", and "best practices". The relevance of each ethos is in particular put in perspective with sense of urgency. This must have us reflected if the ethos of best practices will be the most relevant in the face of climate urgency.

[2] https://www.smartermedicine.ch/fr/liste-top-5/medecine-intensive

> A common concern expressed across interviews, especially by nurses who worked in Covid-19 wards, was that what would ordinarily be considered 'best practice' was not always possible in the pandemic context due to insufficient knowledge and resources. Instead, health-care workers had to prioritize what could or needed to be done: *'We would only address urgent needs. [...] We just felt like we were trying to get by'.* (Harrison et al., 2023)

This approach was framed as a "disaster" model of care.

> Doing best practice, in practice, can thus be summed up as a situated yet iterative process of making care work in relation with what can be known, what can be done, and what can be done better. (here, now, and for now)

As many environmentalists agree (and more and more healthcare workers), we are in a state of environmental emergency that justifies changes in the definition of the good enough. Although it would be possible to picture a very clear distinction between best practices and good enough in certain cases (e.g., using the full surgical hand scrub (soap, water, brush, timed procedure) between patients vs using alcohol-based hand rubs), the exact criteria about the border between good enough and other ethos is in many cases "flurry" (Harrison et al., 2023, p. 5).

Mapping of Imaginaries

Imaginaries are far from being monolithic. Rather, they are composed of several sub-imaginaries for which actors struggle for hegemony, following a Gramscian perspective. In the field of healthcare, one could oppose a dominant one centered on technology, fixing, resource blindness with another one focused on interdependence, slowness, planetary health, and ethical futurity (Puig de la Bellacasa, 2013). This means that what was created as a new magma, as an episteme of modern conditions in healthcare narrative (single-use, more is better, health is curative) can be unmade. In that sense, Castoriadis offers us some tools with his *radical imaginary,* which represents the unique human capacity to create new social meanings, new institutions, and new forms of caring. Hocini and Dallaporta's "poetics of care" offers one example, proposing healing not as a return to prior states but as the emergence of new ways of life. When dividing imaginaries as conflicting sub-imaginaries, for instance, one that would be maximalist and one that would be minimalist, without surprise, the former takes more room in the bibliography than the latter. Trying to characterize an imaginary is far from trivial, yet one can derive manifestations of the imaginary through what is valued in the publication. Given that different imaginaries can be conceived as teleoaffective structures backed by ends and values (Schatzki, 2002), it is possible to extract a set of values of narratives (Stibbe, 2023) that are constitutive of the imaginaries. Below is a set of pillars that are carrying each imaginary (Table 5.7).

The ratios show that in each case the number of publications in the maximalist imaginary is superior to the number of publications in the minimalist imaginary. However, there are wide disparities depending on the pair of items which is observed. The ratio is only about two when comparing the larger cure vs care, goes up to 4 to 5 when observing action, decision logic, and temporal orientation. In other words, the differences are more important when considering what is actually being used on the field than in philosophical terms. Another way to distinguish sub-imaginaries would

Table 5.7 maximalist vs minimalist imaginaries

Dimension	Maximalist imaginary	Article count	Minimalist imaginary	Article count	Ratio
Relation to health	Cure	2,900,000	Care	1,338,000	2.2
Action	"More is better"	219	« Good enough »	55	4.0
Decision logic	Do more	157	Do better	33	4.8
Temporal Orientation	Present	668	Future	132	5.1

Source Pubmed. Dates: all. See details in Appendix A

be, following (Ricoeur, 2013) to distinguish on one axis *reproductive imagination*, which reiterates existing forms, with *productive imagination*, which brings forth new possibilities. The second axis distinguishes *critical distance*, where imagination questions and reframes reality, from *non-critical involvement*, where it remains absorbed in prevailing logics (Fig. 5.2).

Taken together, these four positions present different types of imaginaries. At the bottom left lies the *trace* of maximalism, where "more is better" dominates. At the top left, a *portrait* reframes current practices, such as efficiency or smarter medicine, without radically transforming them. At the top right stands the *novel*, where planetary care imaginaries open new horizons for ethics and environmental preservation. At the bottom right, one finds *illusions*, where technophilic promises of green innovation mask structural inertia. Success requires careful alignment between

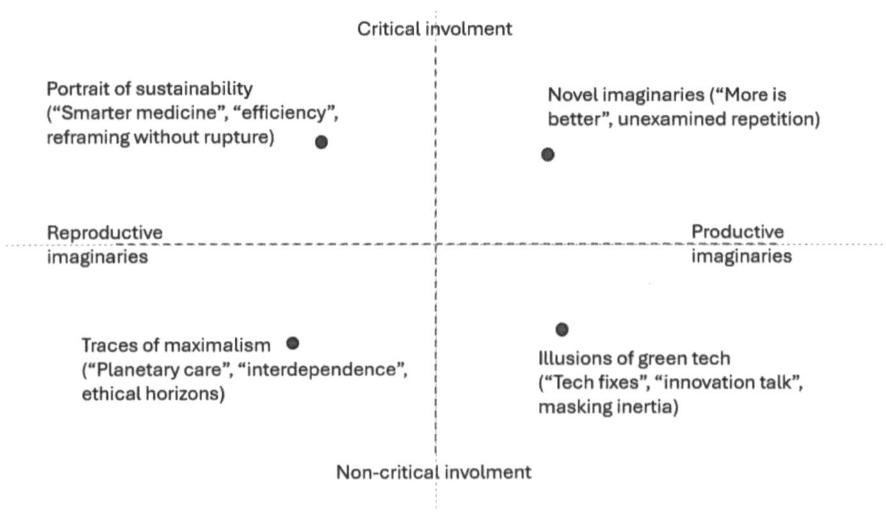

Fig. 5.2 Different forms of imaginaries

eco-friendly technologies and organizational practices, as misalignment between green facilities and outdated behaviors among healthcare professionals often leads to project failures (Pinzone et al., 2016).

What Barriers

One way to see the headwinds that are faced by the different types of innovation is to define 12 barriers at the macro, meso, and micro levels (full description in appendix). When aggregating barriers at the macro (economic incentives, policy gaps, supply chain lock-in, cultural paradigm), meso (temporal urgency, organizational silos, guidelines and power dynamics), and micro-level (training gaps, competing priorities, professional identity, psychological distance), the most radical change in innovation with the most promising gains in terms of environmental impacts (frugal and cultural innovation) face the most resistance, with frugal innovation and cultural innovation cumulating 11 out of 12 barriers. These are represented in Table 5.8.

Enabling Transformation

Now that we have identified barriers to innovation, it becomes possible to make some propositions to lift them.

Beyond Barriers to Innovation

Combine Various Forms of Innovation.

As for interprofessionality, multi-type innovation is one way to avoid separating innovations and to build coalitions that can move toward resource efficiency, starting with the most acceptable forms (technological) to the most challenging ones (frugal, cultural). Technological innovations (which face only 3 barriers in the previous part) provide immediate visible wins (energy reduction, waste decrease). These quick successes generate political capital and resources supporting forms of innovation with slightly more resistance, such as process innovations (optimized sterilization workflows, supply chain redesign) which face 7 barriers, normalizing sustainability considerations in daily practice. Organizational innovation (creating sustainability governance structures, cross-departmental coordination) addresses 8 barriers by establishing accountability mechanisms and reducing silos, providing leverage for deeper changes. Then it becomes possible to address cultural innovation (planetary health education, professional training integrating environmental literacy) which

Table 5.8 barriers per type of innovation

Level	Barrier	Technological	Process	Frugal	Clinical	Organizational	Financial	Service	Social	Cultural
Macro	Economic mis-incentives		**X**	**X**		**X**	**X**	**X**	**X**	**X**
Macro	Policy and regulatory gaps	**X**	**X**	**X**	**X**	**X**	**X**	**X**		**X**
Macro	Supply chain lock-in	**X**	**X**	**X**		**X**				
Macro	Cultural paradigms			**X**	**X**			**X**	**X**	**X**
Meso	Temporal architecture of urgency		**X**	**X**	**X**	**X**		**X**		**X**
Meso	Organizational silos		**X**			**X**	**X**	**X**	**X**	**X**
Meso	Ambivalence of guidelines		**X**	**X**	**X**	**X**				**X**
Meso	Power dynamics			**X**	**X**	**X**			**X**	**X**
Micro	Professional training gaps			**X**	**X**			**X**	**X**	**X**
Micro	Competing priorities		**X**	**X**	**X**	**X**		**X**		**X**
Micro	Professional identities	**X**		**X**	**X**				**X**	**X**
Micro	Cognitive biases & psychological distance			**X**	**X**				**X**	**X**
Total	Barriers per innovation type:	**3**	**7**	**11**	**9**	**8**	**3**	**7**	**7**	**11**

Source Author

confronts 6 barriers. Finally, frugal innovation (adopting materially simpler alternatives like zeerpot refrigeration or mosquito net hernia repair) faces 11 out of 12 barriers but becomes feasible through technological legitimacy, operationalization, sustainability-friendly governance and cultural shifts.

Building Evidence

Clinical validation establishing non-inferiority, demonstrating co-benefits reduces professional resistance by addressing safety concerns while revealing indirect advantages. For instance, portable ultrasound shows accuracy comparable to typical hospital systems for some applications such as trauma assessment, cardiac function, and pregnancy monitoring. Simultaneously, portability, immediate point-of-care availability, resilience with fewer electronic failure points in demanding environments, and reduced infrastructure requirements for rural settings are additional benefits. Similarly, the fact that home-based peritoneal dialysis showed equivalent survival rates with superior quality-of-life metrics challenged assumptions that decentralized care is less effective than hospital care. To show that frugality or simplicity can bring decisive advantages, one must operate strategically by targeting receptive contexts where specific advantages are obvious (e.g., emergency medicine values portability or patients value home-based care) then generate comparative evidence addressing skeptics' concerns and leverage early adopters as champions within professional networks. Evidence generation proves particularly effective against competing priorities barriers, when "safety above all" dominates professional culture, demonstrating that simpler or decentralized approaches maintain safety while offering additional benefits reframes simplicity from compromise to elegant sufficiency.

Professional Education and Training.

Professional education addressing environmental literacy, systems thinking, and planetary health directly confronts training gaps, the one barrier that affects all nine innovation types. Despite marginal recent improvements, medical and health curricula are still full of biomedical content, much less so of environmental health, ecological impacts of clinical decisions, and planetary boundaries. This produces professionals with clinical tunnel vision who cannot recognize healthcare's environmental footprint and room for improvement. Improving environmental literacy reduces professional identity barriers by reframing sustainability from secondary to core clinical skill, in the same way evidence-based medicine became legitimized professional knowledge. Education also addresses psychological distance by making abstract future environmental harms concrete and proximate: when clinicians understand that unnecessary diagnostic testing, overtreatment, and resource-intensive interventions directly harm planetary health affecting patient populations, temporal and spatial distance collapse, making long-term harm very concrete.

Embrace Silent Innovation

Silent innovation (also sometimes mentioned as "invisible innovation") is not a much discussed topics except for a few exceptions (Fuglsang, 2010; Tonkonoff, 2013). It is not totally absent from the healthcare sector (Saidi et al., 2021), where the author acknowledges that

> Innovation activities in health care are difficult to monitor and manage as they are often tied to improvements of ongoing practices and services. Finding a way to make 'hidden innovations' visible is important if innovation is to be managed strategically within and across hospitals (p. 725)

Silent innovation is an old tradition in many sectors already described by Adam Smith in *The Wealth of Nations*. Silent innovations emerge from daily practice experience rather than from formal R&D processes. They are typically motivated by professional values and environmental concerns rather than institutional mandates or economic incentives. Most importantly, they remain largely undocumented in academic literature, institutional reports, or formal innovation tracking systems. In order to recognize silent innovations, innovation systems must recognize organizational and social innovations as equally important as technological interventions.

While innovation is often associated with technological breakthroughs or formal institutional projects, much of the environmental progress occurring in healthcare today is not labeled as such. Drawing on von Hippel's work on "democratizing innovation" and Fuglsang's analysis of "everyday innovation", we identify a crucial category of change that remains largely invisible to formal innovation systems. Many healthcare initiatives might represent innovation without healthcare workers stating it or even realizing it, in the same way Molière's Monsieur Jourdain had been performing prose for his whole life without knowing it. Whether they don't realize it or lack time to have it recognized as such, many healthcare workers are quietly modifying practices to reduce their ecological footprint, without necessarily labeling these acts as "innovation". Part of this has to do with the indicators used, as "non-technological innovation" (like new care pathways or professional role reconfigurations) may be less frequently named in publications not because it happens less, quite the contrary, but because it is less perceived as innovation. However, solutions developed for resource-constrained settings subsequently adopted in high-income contexts, bypass cultural paradigm barriers by demonstrating that simplicity can prove superior even where resources are abundant. This legitimation effect proves particularly powerful against colonial bias, the Global South becomes recognized as innovation source rather than mere recipient. East African products (e.g., zeerpot) or Indian high-volume eye surgery centers' frugal techniques (Aravind model achieving quality outcomes at 1/30th cost) demonstrate that resource constraints drive innovations valuable beyond their original context.

Silent Innovation in Practice

Swiss Maternity Unit Resource Optimization: A team of midwives in a mid-size Swiss hospital in Neuchâtel initiated systematic reduction of disposable items through modified sterilization routines and transition to reusable materials. Because they are not interested in selling it to the outside, they haven't documented through indicators, which is what anyone seeking strategic positioning would do. Discussing the before and after, we estimate that they have reduced by 40% the disposable items over 18 months while maintaining clinical quality indicators. Staff did not consider themselves "innovators", nor are they seeking for an award, they felt this was simply "the right thing to do".

Beyond Urgency and Human Worlds

Temporal orientations have been studied in a wide variety of contexts, in particular in inter-cultural comparisons (Zimbardo & Boyd, 2015), less so between sectors or jobs. Time-as-a-stressor was often considered (see, e.g., Siebenhüner et al., 2020; Wang, 2019), including in the care context, counter-models such as future orientations seem to be less present in the literature. Biomedical care typically operates through urgent, short-term timeframes that correspond to individual biological processes but the longer ecological timescales (climate change, environmental degradation, ecological health) are typically absent. According to Latour, "the Moderns are not creatures who look forward, but who look only at the present, confusing it with reality. This is why the eruption of Gaia surprises them so much. Since they have no time, they are too busy to fail to notice that time is escaping them [...] For them, "future" is entirely constituted by their pasts, without any truly realistic or novel dimension. Children of the Enlightenment, they were accustomed to rejecting with courage and determination the past from which they came, but they never had the habit of inventing the future".[3]

In healthcare settings in which time poverty is often experienced, sustainability initiatives fail because they require what Bateson called "Learning III", a meta-level reflection that enables practitioners to see beyond immediate operational pressures to consider longer-term environmental consequences. Transforming healthcare's environmental impact requires more than technical fixes or policy mandates; it demands what Govindarajan calls "self-disruption" by established healthcare workers, a willingness to question and reconstruct the temporal logics that currently govern clinical practice. Creating time-conscious sustainability requires reimagining organizational practices and professional norms in order to integrate environmental considerations into the fundamental rhythms and routines of care delivery and professional roles and task allocation in ways that distribute environmental responsibility across care

[3] Own translation

teams. This might involve developing specialized positions, sustainability coordinators, waste reduction specialists, or green procurement officers, who have the time and institutional authority to implement environmentally preferable practices.

Augmenting the time perspective also requires expanding the conceptual boundaries of the current healthcare system. Ethics of environmental health are future-oriented and inclusive of more-than-human worlds. They challenge the separation of clinical responsibility from environmental impact and demand an integrated approach to living well together across not only generations but also species. This requires a reformatting of the dualistic, mechanistic, and reductionistic worldview of the modern healthcare culture (Pietroni & Pietroni, 1996). This echoes what Corine Pelluchon calls a "new enlightenment" (Pelluchon, 2021).

Conclusions

In the Anthropocene, the healthcare sector is seeking solutions to reduce its environmental impact and do its part, years if not decades after other sectors. Whatever the reasons (protect the environment to protect the environment (*primum non nocere*), protect the environment to feel better about one's mission, align personal values with professional values, reputation, costs…), healthcare workers and institutions are looking for solutions. This book has hopefully brought three main contributions to the debate on reducing the environmental burden of the healthcare sector.

The first is the laying out of a framework of innovations in the healthcare sector. Nine forms of innovation were developed in the context of this book (Technological, Service, Clinical, Process, Organizational, Business model, Social, Frugal, Cultural). Some are already endemic of the healthcare sector (e.g., clinical innovation) whereas others are more peripheral (e.g., cultural innovation), but are potential solutions for healthcare workers and institutions seeking pro-environmental changes. None of them is a silver bullet and it is likely that several solutions will be needed to bring the changes that are required to meet the requirements of the Paris agreement for the healthcare systems of the Global North. Technological innovations, often presented as the ultimate forms of innovation will not suffice due to rebound effects, the environmental cost of technology and the magical imaginary that surrounds it. It can contribute to some of the changes needed but other types of innovation (change of use, change of definition, change of norms, change of organizations,…) will also be required. Solutions within the healthcare sector can be used directly while those developed outside must be translated into healthcare contexts and realities. For instance, a business model innovation must fit within the insurance and reimbursement frameworks in which healthcare systems are embedded, often with significant differences across countries.

A second contribution is an analysis of the indicators used to depict innovation on the one hand and environmental impacts on the another hand. The first shows that environmental considerations are largely absent from the most dominant indicators, which focus primarily on the number of patents or publications and rarely account for the environmental burden that they may entail. The second highlights a large tropism on carbon metrics, concentrating the debate on energy while overlooking the material dimension of a sector that depends heavily on a limited number of regions for its supply (mainly Asia for medicines and rare earth, Africa and Latin America for metals). Future perspectives should focus on making invisible innovations more visible in order to shift the narrative toward more environmentally sustainable forms of innovations.

A third contribution is a critical reading of current innovation approaches. It is likely that cultural innovations will also be needed to reduce environmental impacts and achieve Net Zero emissions aligned with the Paris Agreement. After many decades characterized by a maximalist imaginary, it is likely that Western countries will have to embrace some "good enough" imaginary. It is not only about doing just as well; it is also a way to build systems that are more robust. In a world of polycrises, robustness and resilience will become just as important as efficiency which have characterized the neoliberal management approaches guiding healthcare institutions. Robustness and resilience show that simplicity and frugality might become desirable. This is not to topple the traditional paradigms of healthcare system (health first, more is better) but to argue that healthcare systems should be able to operate across multiple paradigms, which is not currently the case. In this sense, healthcare systems in the Global South, long considered second-class systems, offer alternatives. They do not need to be adopted directly, but can provide examples and spaces for reflection for healthcare systems in the Global North. Not only are there alternatives in the Global South, but many options also exist within healthcare systems in the Global North. As they currently operate at the margins of official innovative frameworks, making them more visible in necessary to recognize that healthcare systems can significantly improve their environmental performances by using options that already exist. The good news is that many good examples are already present within healthcare systems; they are simply not visible enough and remain at the margins of silent innovation. Recognizing that much is already being done is one step in this direction. Part of this transformation will also depend on metrics. Goodhart's law tend to lead to a reification of the metrics used. At present, the dominant metrics of innovation are patent-based, industry-driven and competitive. The absence of environmental considerations within the current framework leads to tragedy-of-the-commons-type scenarios, in which each actor has an incentive to exploit shared resources for individual benefit. When innovation metrics instead incorporate collaboration, co-construction, and open source approaches, imaginaries of innovation can shift toward care, social innovation and the recognition of environmental impacts. At present, competitors may not fully realize the urge for change. The challenges ahead will require coalitions of individuals who may not see the world in the same way but who need to roll up their sleeves and work together.

References

Aldridge, M. D., & Kelley, A. S. (2015). The myth regarding the high cost of end-of-life care. *American Journal of Public Health, 105*(12), 2411–2415. https://doi.org/10.2105/AJPH.2015.302889

Apesoa-Varano, E. C. (2007). Educated caring: The emergence of professional identity among nurses. *Qualitative Sociology, 30*(3), 249–274.

Baras, A., De Lucia, S., Senn, N., & Brule, G. (2026). Santé-environnement. Low-tech et high-tech en santé, innover pour le meilleur et pour l'avenir. *Revue Medicale Suisse, 22*(947), 238–240.

Berkun, S. (2010). *The myths of innovation.* O'Reilly Media. https://books.google.fr/books?hl=fr&lr=&id=kPCgnc70MSgC&oi=fnd&pg=PR9&dq=berkun+innovation+aids&ots=Hq0vzL2e6w&sig=WmSRPGv2vXJ8Njz6hpBWV5CkS7g

Boumediene, S. (2016). *La colonisation du savoir.* Une histoire des plantes médicinales du «Nouveau Monde»(1492–1750). https://hal.science/halshs-01999007/

Bourdieu, P. (1988). *Homo academicus.* Stanford University Press. https://books.google.fr/books?hl=fr&lr=&id=hfUR028Z-0kC&oi=fnd&pg=PR10&dq=bourdieu+homo+academicus&ots=xOkqfXlWfX&sig=n8JG556UdqMSfBchXAsDyhB3aJQ

Bourdieu, P., & Wacquant, L. J. (1992). *An invitation to reflexive sociology.* University of Chicago press.. https://books.google.fr/books?hl=fr&lr=&id=rs4fEHa0ijAC&oi=fnd&pg=PR7&dq=(Bourdieu+%26+Wacquant,+1992).&ots=dyLc4HlOKO&sig=eJr9bk6RXh_jhqr7zQ589U_Czm0

Brulé, G., Boiko, P., Mezeray, T. M., Nadal, D., Vuilleumier, S., Senn, N., Fehr, J., Crivelli, L., Zinsstag, J., & Probst-Hensch, N. (2026). Can One Health help reduce the environmental impacts of the healthcare system in Switzerland? Insights from an interdisciplinary focus group. *Ethics, Medicine and Public Health, 34*, 101227.

Canguilhem, G. (1966). *Le normal et le pathologique.*

Cheon, O., Song, M., & Meier, K. J. (2022). Gender differences in performance-driven managerial innovation: Evidence from US nursing homes. *International Public Management Journal, 25*(6), 841–861. https://doi.org/10.1080/10967494.2021.1941454

Çitaku, F., Violato, C., Beran, T., Donnon, T., Hecker, K., & Cawthorpe, D. (2012). Leadership competencies for medical education and healthcare professions: Population-based study. *BMJ Open, 2*(2), e000812.

Dutt Bhardwaj, N., Jain, A., Srivastava, K., Srivastava, P., & Agarwal, K. (2023). Volume of plastics among biomedical waste generated in an Indian healthcare facility: The hidden burden. *International Journal of Scientific Research*, 22–24. https://doi.org/10.36106/ijsr/5806480

Foucault, M. (2002). *The birth of the clinic.* Routledge. https://api.taylorfrancis.com/content/books/mono/download?identifierName=doi&identifierValue=10.4324/9780203406373&type=googlepdf

Fuglsang, L. (2010). Bricolage and invisible innovation in public service innovation. *Journal of Innovation Economics & Management, 5*(1), 67–87.

Gaspar, J.-F., Molina, Y., & Tschopp, F. (2025). *L'intervention sociale aux frontières du médical.* Éditions ies. https://books.google.fr/books?hl=fr&lr=&id=_88-EQAAQBAJ&oi=fnd&pg=PA6&dq=l%27intervention+social+aux+fronti%C3%A8res+du+medication&ots=iGgxkXeOvH&sig=1R_YLX1uVMUCQQREgqzXYgXzZQY

Guien, J. (2025). *Le désir de nouveautés: L'obsolescence au cøeur du capitalisme (XVe-XXIe siècle).* La Découverte.. https://books.google.fr/books?hl=fr&lr=&id=4UpGEQAAQBAJ&oi=fnd&pg=PA1947&dq=jeanne+guien+d%C3%A9sir+de+nouveaut%C3%A9s&ots=vOvUBUMTY5&sig=j8QAo8trfs9NYj-5gOTPYarEDcA

Harris, M., Bhatti, Y., Prime, M., Del Castillo, J., & Parston, G. (2018). Low-cost innovation in healthcare: What you find depends on where you look. *Journal of the Royal Society of Medicine, 111*(2), 47–50. https://doi.org/10.1177/0141076817738501

Harrison, M., Rhodes, T., & Lancaster, K. (2023). Situating'best practice': Making Healthcare familiar and good enough in the face of unknowns. *SSM-Qualitative Research in Health, 4*, 100343.

Illes, J., Perreault, M. L., Bassil, K., Bjaalie, J. G., Taylor-Bragge, R. L., Chneiweiss, H., Gregory, T. R., Kumar, B. N., Matshabane, O. P., & Svalastog, A. L. (2025). Two-Eyed Seeing and other Indigenous perspectives for neuroscience. *Nature, 638*(8049), 58–68.

Ivanović, T., Meisel, H.-J., Som, C., & Nowack, B. (2022). Material flow analysis of single-use plastics in healthcare: A case study of a surgical hospital in Germany. *Resources, Conservation and Recycling, 185*, 106425.

Lehoux, P., Miller, F. A., & Daudelin, G. (2016). How does venture capital operate in medical innovation? *BMJ Innovations, 2*(3) https://innovations.bmj.com/content/2/3/111.abstract

Longchamp, P., Toffel, K., Bühlmann, F., & Tawfik, A. (2015). De la sociologie de l'innovation à l'imagination sociologique. La théorie des champs à l'épreuve de la profession infirmière. *Cahiers de recherche sociologique, 59–60*, 135–156. https://doi.org/10.7202/1036790ar

McNamara, B. (2004). Good enough death: Autonomy and choice in Australian palliative care. *Social Science & Medicine, Good and Bad Death, 58*(5), 929–938. https://doi.org/10.1016/j.socscimed.2003.10.042

Mendonca, J., & Reis, A. (2020). Exploring the mechanisms of gender effects in user innovation. *Technological Forecasting and Social Change, 155*, 119988.

Merchant, C. (2010). *Ecological revolutions: Nature, gender, and science in New England*. University of North Carolina Press. https://books.google.fr/books?hl=fr&lr=&id=FkcyIXUg-o4C&oi=fnd&pg=PR7&dq=merchant+nature&ots=EP4maI3Yvs&sig=AmL9HA1wWJZ_VgexBRkhuyYcpN4

Merchant, C. (2014). The death of nature: Women and ecology in the scientific revolution. In *Earthcare* (pp. 75–90). Routledge. https://www.taylorfrancis.com/chapters/edit/10.4324/9781315021683-6/death-nature-carolyn-merchant

Pelluchon, C. (2021). *Les Lumières à l'âge du vivant*. Seuil. https://books.google.fr/books?hl=fr&lr=&id=lWcOEAAAQBAJ&oi=fnd&pg=PT5&dq=pelluchon+lumi%C3%A8res&ots=gYhpoRYXi4&sig=9zvAdooQctMzcAkYJNNNLWEjlB0

Pietroni, P., & Pietroni, C. (1996). Innovation in community care and primary health: The Marylebone experiment. *(No Title)*. https://cir.nii.ac.jp/crid/1130000794209891968

Pinzone, M., Guerci, M., Lettieri, E., & Redman, T. (2016). Progressing in the change journey towards sustainability in healthcare: The role of 'Green'HRM. *Journal of Cleaner Production, 122*, 201–211.

Plochg, T., & Hamer, S. (2012). Innovation more than an artefact? Conceptualizing the effects of drawing medicine into management. *International Journal of Healthcare Management, 5*(4), 189–192. https://doi.org/10.1179/2047971912Y.0000000019

Puig de La Bellacasa, M. (2013). *Politiques féministes et construction des savoirs: «Penser nous devons"!* https://www.torrossa.com/it/resources/an/5122996

Ragasa, C. (2012). *Gender and institutional dimensions of agricultural technology adoption: A review of literature and synthesis of 35 case studies*. https://ageconsearch.umn.edu/record/126747/.

Ramos, T. M., Christensen, T. B., Bour, A., Almroth, B. C., Kristensen, D. M., Selck, H., & Syberg, K. (2023). A not so circular healthcare economy: A review of challenges with plastic associated chemicals. *TrAC Trends in Analytical Chemistry, 166*, 117191.

Ricoeur, P. (2013). *Du texte à l'action. Essais d'herméneutique, t. 2* (Vol. 2). Média Diffusion. https://books.google.fr/books?hl=fr&lr=&id=u-M9AgAAQBAJ&oi=fnd&pg=PT5&dq=ricoeur+Du+texte+%C3%A0+l%27action.+Essais+d%27herm%C3%A9neutique+II&ots=gKkU7h2kaV&sig=WLsvl_kzCuUai3UTUZoD5SPsj1s

Rosa, H. (2003). Social acceleration: ethical and political consequences of a desynchronized high–speed society. *Constellations: An International Journal of Critical & Democratic Theory, 10*(1).

Saidi, T., Thune, T. M., & Bugge, M. (2021). Making 'hidden innovation' visible? A case study of an innovation management system in health care. *Technology Analysis & Strategic Management, 33*(7), 729–741. https://doi.org/10.1080/09537325.2020.1841156

Schatzki, T. R. (2002). *The site of the social: A philosophical account of the constitution of social life and change.* Penn State Press.

Schøtt, T., & Cheraghi, M. (2015). Gendering pursuits of innovation: Embeddedness in networks and culture. *International Journal of Entrepreneurship and Small Business, 24*(1), 83. https://doi.org/10.1504/IJESB.2015.066160

Siebenhüner, K., Battegay, E., & Hämmig, O. (2020). Temporal work stressors and satisfaction with work, life and health among health professionals in Switzerland. *Swiss Medical Weekly, 150*, w20175.

Sivaram, S., Roy, A., & Ray, S. K. (2021). The paradox of plastics in healthcare and health. In *Climate change and the health sector* (pp. 215–223). Routledge India. https://www.taylorfrancis.com/chapters/oa-edit/10.4324/9781003190516-26/paradox-plastics-healthcare-health-swaminathan-sivaram-aditi-roy-swapan-ray

Stibbe, A. (2023). *Econarrative.* https://www.torrossa.com/gs/resourceProxy?an=5605517&publisher=FZ0661.

Tonkonoff, S. (2013). A new social physic: The sociology of Gabriel Tarde and its legacy. *Current Sociology, 61*(3), 267–282. https://doi.org/10.1177/0011392113477578

Van Wijngaarden, J. D. H., Botje, D., Ilinca, S., Van Der Waa, N., Mendes, R. V., Hamer, S., & Plochg, T. (2012). How doctor involvement in management affects innovation. *International Journal of Healthcare Management, 5*(4), 203–207. https://doi.org/10.1179/2047971912Y.0000000021

Wang, C. (2019). Temporal dynamics in the daily lives of health practitioners. *Time & Society, 28*(4), 1552–1576. https://doi.org/10.1177/0961463X18787047

Winders, J., & Smith, B. E. (2019). Social reproduction and capitalist production: A genealogy of dominant imaginaries. *Progress in Human Geography, 43*(5), 871–889. https://doi.org/10.1177/0309132518791730

Zhou, G., & Xu, J. (2007). Adoption of educational technology: How does gender matter? *International Journal of Teaching and Learning in Higher Education, 19*(2), 140–153.

Zimbardo, P. G., & Boyd, J. N. (2015). Putting time in perspective: A valid, reliable individual-differences metric. In M. Stolarski, N. Fieulaine, & W. Van Beek (Eds.), *Time perspective theory; Review, research and application* (pp. 17–55). Springer International Publishing. https://doi.org/10.1007/978-3-319-07368-2_2

Appendix A
Search Equation

We wish to thank Natacha Bossi, professional librarian and the library of Geneva School of Health Sciences, for reading, verifying and proposing solutions for the whole bibliometric analysis. The work would not be so robust without her laser eye.

Environmental Measures Used

Methodological approach	Search terms used	Results
Carbon footprint	((“sustainable healthcare"[Title/Abstract] OR “healthcare sustainability"[Title/Abstract] OR “green healthcare"[Title/Abstract])) AND ((Carbon Footprint[MeSH Terms]) OR (Carbon Footprint*[Title/Abstract]))	73
Life Cycle Assessment (LCA)	((“sustainable healthcare"[Title/Abstract] OR “healthcare sustainability"[Title/Abstract] OR “green healthcare"[Title/Abstract])) AND ((Carbon Footprint[MeSH Terms]) OR (Carbon Footprint*[Title/Abstract]))	21
Ecological footprint	((“sustainable healthcare"[Title/Abstract] OR “healthcare sustainability"[Title/Abstract] OR “green healthcare"[Title/Abstract])) AND ((Carbon Footprint[MeSH Terms]) OR (Carbon Footprint*[Title/Abstract]))	5
Pharmaceutical pollution	((“sustainable healthcare"[Title/Abstract] OR “healthcare sustainability"[Title/Abstract] OR “green healthcare"[Title/Abstract])) AND (“pharmaceutical pollution"[Title/Abstract] OR “drug pollution"[Title/Abstract] OR “pharmaceutical residues"[Title/Abstract] OR “drug residues"[Title/Abstract])	3

G. Brulé, *Reducing the Environmental Impact of Healthcare Systems*, Sustainable Business Development, https://doi.org/10.1007/978-3-032-34889-0

Indicators Used

Resource/Impact	Input Equation	Process Equation	Output Equation
	14	42	118
Materials	(green healthcare[Title/Abstract] OR "healthcare sustainability"[Title/Abstract] OR sustainable healthcare[Title/Abstract]) AND (Equipment and Supplies[MeSH Terms] OR material*[Title/Abstract] OR medical device*[Title/Abstract] OR procurement*[Title/Abstract] OR supply chain*[Title/Abstract]) AND (consumption*[Title/Abstract] OR input*[Title/Abstract] OR purchasing*[Title/Abstract])	(green healthcare[Title/Abstract] OR "healthcare sustainability"[Title/Abstract] OR sustainable healthcare[Title/Abstract]) AND (Equipment and Supplies[MeSH Terms] OR "material*"[Title/Abstract] OR "equipment"[Title/Abstract] OR "device*"[Title/Abstract]) AND ("reus*"[Title/Abstract] OR "sterilization"[Title/Abstract] OR "single-use"[Title/Abstract] OR "reprocessing"[Title/Abstract])	(green healthcare[Title/Abstract] OR healthcare sustainability[Title/Abstract] OR sustainable healthcare[Title/Abstract]) AND (Equipment and Supplies[MeSH Terms] OR "material*"[Title/Abstract] OR "solid waste"[Title/Abstract] OR "plastic waste"[Title/Abstract] OR "medical waste"[Title/Abstract])
	29	36	127

(continued)

(continued)

Resource/Impact	Input Equation	Process Equation	Output Equation
Energy/carbon	(green healthcare[Title/Abstract] OR “healthcare sustainability"[Title/Abstract] OR sustainable healthcare[Title/Abstract]) AND (“energy"[Title/Abstract] OR “electricity"[Title/Abstract] OR “fuel"[Title/Abstract]) AND (“input"[Title/Abstract] OR “consumption"[Title/Abstract] OR “demand"[Title/Abstract])	(green healthcare[Title/Abstract] OR healthcare sustainability[Title/Abstract] OR sustainable healthcare[Title/Abstract]) AND (“energy"[Title/Abstract] OR “HVAC"[Title/Abstract] OR “operating room*"[Title/Abstract] OR “ventilation"[Title/Abstract]) AND (“efficiency"[Title/Abstract] OR “management"[Title/Abstract] OR “optimization"[Title/Abstract])	(green healthcare[Title/Abstract] OR healthcare sustainability[Title/Abstract] OR sustainable healthcare[Title/Abstract]) AND (Carbon Footprint[MeSH Terms] OR “carbon footprint*"[Title/Abstract] OR CO2[Title/Abstract] OR “GHG emission*"[Title/Abstract] OR “greenhouse gas*"[Title/Abstract])
	23	3	17
Water	(green healthcare[Title/Abstract] OR “healthcare sustainability"[Title/Abstract] OR sustainable healthcare[Title/Abstract]) AND (“water"[Title/Abstract]) AND (“consumption"[Title/Abstract] OR “demand*"[Title/Abstract] OR “input"[Title/Abstract] OR “use"[Title/Abstract])	(green healthcare[Title/Abstract] OR “healthcare sustainability"[Title/Abstract] OR sustainable healthcare[Title/Abstract]) AND (“water"[Title/Abstract]) AND (“dialysis"[Title/Abstract] OR “sterilization"[Title/Abstract] OR “cooling"[Title/Abstract] OR “laundry"[Title/Abstract])	(green healthcare[Title/Abstract] OR healthcare sustainability[Title/Abstract] OR sustainable healthcare[Title/Abstract]) AND (Carbon Footprint[MeSH Terms] OR “carbon footprint*"[Title/Abstract] OR CO2[Title/Abstract] OR “GHG emission*"[Title/Abstract] OR “greenhouse gas*"[Title/Abstract])
	35	31	42

(continued)

(continued)

Resource/Impact	Input Equation	Process Equation	Output Equation
Pharmaceuticals/ chemicals	(green healthcare[Title/ Abstract] OR healthcare sustainability[Title/ Abstract] OR sustainable healthcare[Title/ Abstract]) AND (Carbon Footprint[MeSH Terms] OR "carbon footprint*"[Title/ Abstract] OR CO2[Title/Abstract] OR "GHG emission*"[Title/ Abstract] OR "greenhouse gas*"[Title/Abstract])	(green healthcare[Title/ Abstract] OR "healthcare sustainability"[Title/ Abstract] OR sustainable healthcare[Title/ Abstract]) AND ("pharmaceutical*"[Title/ Abstract] OR "prescrib*"[Title/ Abstract] OR "antibiotic*"[Title/ Abstract] OR "anesthetic gas*"[Title/Abstract]) AND ("practice*"[Title/ Abstract] OR "stewardship"[Title/ Abstract] OR "choice*"[Title/Abstract] OR "rational use"[Title/ Abstract])	(green healthcare[Title/ Abstract] OR healthcare sustainability[Title/ Abstract] OR sustainable healthcare[Title/ Abstract]) AND ("pharmaceutical*"[Title/ Abstract] OR "drug*"[Title/Abstract] OR "anesthetic gas*"[Title/Abstract]) AND ("pollution"[Title/ Abstract] OR "residue*"[Title/ Abstract] OR "environmental*"[Title/ Abstract] OR "wastewater*"[Title/ Abstract] OR "emission*"[Title/ Abstract])

Targets of Impacts-Reducing Initiatives

Category	Search equation	Article Count
Patient/Clinical	("healthcare innovation*"[Title/Abstract] OR "health innovation*"[Title/Abstract] OR "medical innovation*"[Title/ Abstract]) AND ("patient outcome*"[Title/Abstract] OR "clinical benefit*"[Title/Abstract] OR "quality"[Title/Abstract] OR "effectiveness"[Title/Abstract] OR "efficiency"[Title/Abstract] OR "Quality of Health Care"[MeSH Terms] OR Efficiency[MeSH Terms] OR Treatment Outcome*[Title/Abstract])	1150
Social	(("healthcare innovation*"[Title/Abstract] OR "health innovation*"[Title/Abstract] OR "medical innovation*"[Title/ Abstract])) AND (("social benefit*"[Title/Abstract] OR "equity"[Title/Abstract] OR "communit*"[Title/Abstract] OR "social determinant* of health"[Title/Abstract] OR "Health service* accessibility"[Title/Abstract] OR "social justice"[Title/Abstract] OR "Health Inequit*"[Title/Abstract] OR "healthcare disparit*"[Title/ Abstract] OR "Health statu* disparit*"[Title/Abstract] OR "Social Determinants of Health"[MeSH Terms] OR "Health Services Accessibility"[MeSH Terms] OR "Social Justice"[MeSH Terms] OR "Health Inequities"[MeSH Terms]))	524

(continued)

(continued)

Category	Search equation	Article Count
Economic	((“healthcare innovation*"[Title/Abstract] OR “health innovation*"[Title/Abstract] OR “medical innovation*"[Title/Abstract])) AND (“cost–benefit analys*"[Title/Abstract] OR “cost-effectiv*"[Title/Abstract] OR “economic benefit*"[Title/Abstract] OR “efficienc*"[Title/Abstract] OR “cost reduction"[Title/Abstract] OR “Cost Saving*"[Title/Abstract] OR “Value-Based Purchasing"[Title/Abstract] OR “cost analys*"[Title/Abstract] OR “Health care cost*"[Title/Abstract] OR “Economics, Medical"[MeSH Terms] OR “Costs and Cost Analysis"[MeSH Terms] OR “Value-Based Purchasing"[MeSH Terms] OR “Efficiency"[MeSH Terms] OR “Cost Savings"[MeSH Terms])	348
Environmental	((“healthcare innovation*"[Title/Abstract] OR “health innovation*"[Title/Abstract] OR “medical innovation*"[Title/Abstract])) AND ((“environmental"[Title/Abstract] OR “Climate Chang*"[Title/Abstract] OR “Waste management"[Title/Abstract] OR “sustainability"[Title/Abstract] OR “carbon"[Title/Abstract] OR “green*"[Title/Abstract] OR “ecological*"[Title/Abstract] OR “sustainable development"[Title/Abstract] OR “Environmental Health"[MeSH Terms] OR “Conservation of Natural Resources"[MeSH Terms] OR “Climate Change"[MeSH Terms] OR “Waste Management"[MeSH Terms] OR “Environmental Pollution"[MeSH Terms]))	227

The 5Rs Strategy

Strategy	PubMed search equation	Results
Refuse	(("sustainable healthcare"[Title/Abstract] OR "healthcare sustainability"[Title/Abstract] OR "green healthcare"[Title/Abstract])) AND (("overuse"[Title/Abstract] OR "unnecessary care"[Title/Abstract] OR "low-value care"[Title/Abstract] OR "overtreatment"[Title/Abstract] OR "de-prescrib*"[Title/Abstract] OR "deprescrib*"[Title/Abstract] OR "choosing wisely"[Title/Abstract] OR "overdiagnos*"[Title/Abstract] OR Medical Overuse[MeSH Terms]))	31
Reduce	("sustainable healthcare"[Title/Abstract] OR "healthcare sustainability"[Title/Abstract] OR "green healthcare"[Title/Abstract]) AND ("resource reduction"[Title/Abstract] OR "energy efficien*"[Title/Abstract] OR "waste reduction"[Title/Abstract] OR "reducing consumption"[Title/Abstract])	24
Reuse	("sustainable healthcare"[Title/Abstract] OR "healthcare sustainability"[Title/Abstract] OR "green healthcare"[Title/Abstract]) AND ("reus*"[Title/Abstract] OR "equipment reuse"[Title/Abstract] OR "single-use"[Title/Abstract])	52

(continued)

(continued)

Strategy	PubMed search equation	Results
Rethink	("sustainable healthcare"[Title/Abstract] OR "healthcare sustainability"[Title/Abstract] OR "green healthcare"[Title/Abstract]) AND ("rethink*"[Title/Abstract] OR "care model innovation"[Title/Abstract] OR "system redesign"[Title/Abstract] OR "healthcare transformation"[Title/Abstract] OR "reimagin*"[Title/Abstract] OR "care pathway*"[Title/Abstract])	31
Recycle	("sustainable healthcare"[Title/Abstract] OR "healthcare sustainability"[Title/Abstract] OR "green healthcare"[Title/Abstract]) AND ("recycl*"[Title/Abstract] OR "waste segregation"[Title/Abstract] OR "waste management"[Title/Abstract] OR "medical waste"[Title/Abstract] OR "healthcare waste"[Title/Abstract] OR "hospital waste"[Title/Abstract] OR Recycling[MeSH Terms])	77

Imaginaries

Dimension	Maximalist Imaginary	Minimalist Imaginary					Ratio
Relation to health	Cure	Care	("cure*"[Title/Abstract] OR "treatment*"[Title/Abstract] OR "therap*"[Title/Abstract] OR "intervention*"[Title/Abstract]) AND ("healthcare"[Title/Abstract] OR "medicine"[Title/Abstract] OR "clinical"[Title/Abstract])	("care"[Title/Abstract] OR "caring"[Title/Abstract] OR "support*"[Title/Abstract] OR "nurs*"[Title/Abstract]) AND ("healthcare"[Title/Abstract] OR "medicine"[Title/Abstract] OR "clinical"[Title/Abstract])	2,900,000	1,338,000	2.2
Action	"More is better"	« Good enough»	("interventionist care"[Title/Abstract] OR "active treatment"[Title/Abstract] OR "medical action"[Title/Abstract]) AND (clinical outcomes[Title/Abstract] OR health delivery[Title/Abstract])	("clinical discernment"[Title/Abstract] OR "watchful waiting"[Title/Abstract] OR "non-intervention"[Title/Abstract]) AND ("patient-centered care"[Title/Abstract] OR "general practice"[Title/Abstract])	219	55	4.0

(continued)

(continued)

Dimension	Maximalist Imaginary	Minimalist Imaginary					Ratio
Decision logic	Do more	Do better	(("sustainable healthcare"[Title/Abstract] OR "healthcare sustainability"[Title/Abstract] OR "green healthcare"[Title/Abstract]) AND ("do more"[Title/Abstract] OR "doing more"[Title/Abstract] OR "scal* up"[Title/Abstract] OR "expansion"[Title/Abstract] OR "comprehensive*"[Title/Abstract] OR "intensive"[Title/Abstract] OR "aggressive treatment"[Title/Abstract] OR "maximi*"[Title/Abstract]))	((“sustainable healthcare"[Title/Abstract] OR “healthcare sustainability"[Title/Abstract] OR “green healthcare"[Title/Abstract]) AND (“minimiz*"[Title/Abstract] OR “parsimoni*"[Title/Abstract] OR “simplif*"[Title/Abstract] OR “sobri*"[Title/Abstract] OR “frugal"[Title/Abstract]))	157	33	4.8
Temporal orientation	Present	Future	("urgent intervention"[Title/Abstract] OR "rapid response"[Title/Abstract] OR "time-sensitive treatment"[Title/Abstract]) AND ("healthcare"[Title/Abstract] OR "emergency care"[Title/Abstract])	(“anticipatory care"[Title/Abstract] OR “preventive ethics"[Title/Abstract] OR “long-term planning"[Title/Abstract]) AND (“healthcare"[Title/Abstract] OR “primary care"[Title/Abstract])	668	132	5.1

The 9-Innovation Framework

Innovation subtype	Sustainability-focused PubMed equation	
Technological	((“sustainable healthcare"[Title/Abstract] OR “green healthcare"[Title/Abstract]) AND (“technolog*"[Title/Abstract] OR “device*"[Title/Abstract] OR “equipment"[Title/Abstract] OR “digital health"[Title/Abstract] OR Technology[MeSH Terms] OR Equipment and Supplies[MeSH Terms]))	197
Process	((“sustainable healthcare"[Title/Abstract] OR “green healthcare"[Title/Abstract]) AND (“process innovation"[Title/Abstract] OR “workflow"[Title/Abstract] OR “lean"[Title/Abstract] OR “supply chain"[Title/Abstract]))	17
Frugal	((“sustainable healthcare"[Title/Abstract] OR “green healthcare"[Title/Abstract]) AND (“frugal innovation"[Title/Abstract] OR “low-cost"[Title/Abstract] OR “appropriate technology"[Title/Abstract] OR “resource-constrained"[Title/Abstract] OR “jugaad"[Title/Abstract]))	13
Clinical	((“sustainable healthcare"[Title/Abstract] OR “green healthcare"[Title/Abstract]) AND (“care pathway*"[Title/Abstract] OR “clinical practice*"[Title/Abstract] OR Clinical Protocols[MeSH Terms]))	50
Organizational	((“sustainable healthcare"[Title/Abstract] OR “green healthcare"[Title/Abstract]) AND (“care delivery model*"[Title/Abstract] OR “integrated care"[Title/Abstract] OR Organizational Innovation[MeSH Terms]))	11
Financial	((“sustainable healthcare"[Title/Abstract] OR “green healthcare"[Title/Abstract]) AND (“financial innovation"[Title/Abstract] OR “payment model*"[Title/Abstract] OR “value-based"[Title/Abstract] OR “financing mechanism*"[Title/Abstract]))	19
Service	((“sustainable healthcare"[Title/Abstract] OR “green healthcare"[Title/Abstract]) AND (“service innovation"[Title/Abstract] OR “telehealth"[Title/Abstract] OR “home care"[Title/Abstract] OR “mobile health"[Title/Abstract] OR Telemedicine[MeSH Terms] OR Home Care Services[MeSH Terms] OR e-health[Title/Abstract]))	31
Social	((“sustainable healthcare"[Title/Abstract] OR “green healthcare"[Title/Abstract]) AND (“social innovation"[Title/Abstract] OR “community health*"[Title/Abstract] OR “patient engagement"[Title/Abstract] OR Patient Participation[MeSH Terms]))	17
Cultural	((“sustainable healthcare"[Title/Abstract] OR “green healthcare"[Title/Abstract]) AND (“cultural change"[Title/Abstract] OR “behavior* chang*"[Title/Abstract] OR “behaviour* change"[Title/Abstract] OR “paradigm shift"[Title/Abstract]))	21

Analysis of First Author Institutional Affiliations for Environmental Healthcare Innovation

Search: (((“Ambulatory Care” [Mesh] OR “Delivery of Health Care"[Mesh] OR “Home Care Services"[Mesh] OR “Hospitals"[Mesh] OR “Primary Health Care"[Mesh] OR “Telemedicine"[Mesh] OR “ambulatory care*"[Title/Abstract] OR “delivery of health care*"[Title/Abstract] OR “healthcare service*"[Title/Abstract] OR “home care service*"[Title/Abstract] OR “hospital*"[Title/Abstract] OR “primary health care*"[Title/Abstract] OR “telemedicine*"[Title/Abstract])) AND ((“Carbon Footprint"[Mesh] OR “Environmental Pollutants"[Mesh] OR “Greenhouse Gases"[Mesh] OR “Medical Waste"[Mesh] OR “Waste Management"[Mesh] OR “carbon footprint*"[Title/Abstract] OR “ecological footprint*"[Title/Abstract] OR “energy consumption*"[Title/Abstract] OR “energy efficien*"[Title/Abstract] OR “energy use*"[Title/Abstract] OR “environmental footprint*"[Title/Abstract] OR “environmental pollutant*"[Title/Abstract] OR “greenhouse gas*"[Title/Abstract] OR “medical wast*"[Title/Abstract] OR “waste generation*"[Title/Abstract] OR “waste management*"[Title/Abstract] OR “waste segregation*"[Title/Abstract]))) AND ((“Equipment Reuse"[Mesh] OR “Recycling"[Mesh] OR “Refuse Disposal"[Mesh] OR “energy efficienc*"[Title/Abstract] OR “equipment reus*"[Title/Abstract] OR “green initiativ*"[Title/Abstract] OR “green practice*"[Title/Abstract] OR “recycle"[Title/Abstract] OR “reduction*"[Title/Abstract] OR “refuse disposal*"[Title/Abstract] OR “repurpose"[Title/Abstract] OR “reuse"[Title/Abstract] OR “smarter medicin*"[Title/Abstract] OR “sustainable practice*"[Title/Abstract])).

Publication period: 2025.

Sample: 187 publications meeting criteria.

Geographic coding based on first author institutional address.

Analysis Per Profession

Title	Equation	Results
Base	("green healthcare"[Title/Abstract] OR "healthcare sustainability"[Title/Abstract] OR "sustainable healthcare"[Title/Abstract])	965
Medical doctors	("green healthcare"[Title/Abstract] OR "healthcare sustainability"[Title/Abstract] OR "sustainable healthcare"[Title/Abstract]) AND (General Practitioners[MeSH Terms]OR General Surgery[MeSH Terms] OR Physicians[MeSH Terms] OR doctor*[Title/Abstract] OR GP[Title/Abstract] OR "medical practitioner*"[Title/Abstract] OR physician*[Title/Abstract] OR surg*[Title/Abstract])	195

(continued)

(continued)

Title	Equation	Results
Nurses	("green healthcare"[Title/Abstract] OR "healthcare sustainability"[Title/Abstract] OR "sustainable healthcare"[Title/Abstract]) AND (Nurses[MeSH Terms] OR Nursing[MeSH Terms] OR Nursing care[MeSH Terms] OR nurs*[Title/Abstract])	98
Pharmacists	("green healthcare"[Title/Abstract] OR "healthcare sustainability"[Title/Abstract] OR "sustainable healthcare"[Title/Abstract]) AND (Pharmacists[MeSH Terms] OR Pharmacy[MeSH Terms] OR pharmacist*[Title/Abstract] OR pharmacy[Title/Abstract])	17
Physiotherapists	("green healthcare"[Title/Abstract] OR "healthcare sustainability"[Title/Abstract] OR "sustainable healthcare"[Title/Abstract]) AND (physical therapy specialty[MeSH Terms] OR physical therapists[MeSH Terms] OR physical therapy modalities[MeSH Terms] OR "physical therap*"[Title/Abstract] OR physiotherap*[Title/Abstract] OR PT[Title/Abstract])	9
Midwives	("green healthcare"[Title/Abstract] OR "healthcare sustainability"[Title/Abstract] OR "sustainable healthcare"[Title/Abstract]) AND ("Midwifery"[MeSH Terms] OR midwi*[Title/Abstract])	8
Radiological imaging	("green healthcare"[Title/Abstract] OR "healthcare sustainability"[Title/Abstract] OR "sustainable healthcare"[Title/Abstract]) AND ("radiology technician*"[Title/Abstract] OR "radiologic technologist*"[Title/Abstract] OR radiographer*[Title/Abstract])	6
Nutritionists	("green healthcare"[Title/Abstract] OR "healthcare sustainability"[Title/Abstract] OR "sustainable healthcare"[Title/Abstract]) AND ("Nutritional Sciences"[MeSH Terms] OR "Nutritionists"[MeSH Terms] OR dietetic*[Title/Abstract] OR dietician*[Title/Abstract] OR nutrition*[Title/Abstract])	16

Analysis of Gender Patterns in Healthcare Innovation Leadership

Sample: 187 recent publications from first half of PubMed 2025 (analysis done in july).

Equation scoping:

((("Ambulatory Care" [Mesh] OR "Delivery of Health Care"[Mesh] OR "Home Care Services"[Mesh] OR "Hospitals"[Mesh] OR "Primary Health Care"[Mesh] OR "Telemedicine"[Mesh] OR "ambulatory care*"[Title/Abstract] OR "delivery of health care*"[Title/Abstract] OR "healthcare service*"[Title/Abstract] OR "home care service*"[Title/Abstract] OR "hospital*"[Title/Abstract] OR "primary health care*"[Title/Abstract] OR "telemedicine*"[Title/Abstract]))

AND (("Carbon Footprint"[Mesh] OR "Environmental Pollutants"[Mesh] OR "Greenhouse Gases"[Mesh] OR "Medical Waste"[Mesh] OR "Waste Management"[Mesh] OR "carbon footprint*"[Title/Abstract] OR "ecological footprint*"[Title/Abstract] OR "energy consumption*"[Title/Abstract] OR "energy efficien*"[Title/Abstract] OR "energy use*"[Title/Abstract] OR "environmental footprint*"[Title/Abstract] OR "environmental pollutant*"[Title/Abstract] OR "greenhouse gas*"[Title/Abstract] OR "medical wast*"[Title/Abstract] OR "waste generation*"[Title/Abstract] OR "waste management*"[Title/Abstract] OR "waste segregation*"[Title/Abstract]))) AND (("Equipment Reuse"[Mesh] OR "Recycling"[Mesh] OR "Refuse Disposal"[Mesh] OR "energy efficienc*"[Title/Abstract] OR "equipment reus*"[Title/Abstract] OR "green initiativ*"[Title/Abstract] OR "green practice*"[Title/Abstract] OR "recycle"[Title/Abstract] OR "reduction*"[Title/Abstract] OR "refuse disposal*"[Title/Abstract] OR "repurpose"[Title/Abstract] OR "reuse"[Title/Abstract] OR "smarter medicin*"[Title/Abstract] OR "sustainable practice*"[Title/Abstract])).

Gender analysis protocol:

1. Genderize API analysis of first author names
2. Manual verification for ambiguous cases using institutional websites
3. Confidence threshold: > 0.70 probability
4. Cultural verification/visual verification on the websites for non-Western names

Table A.1 MESH terms

MeSH Terms	Entry Date	URL
Attitude	1999	https://www.ncbi.nlm.nih.gov/mesh/68001290
Carbon Footprint	2011	https://www.ncbi.nlm.nih.gov/mesh/?term=Carbon+Footprint
Climate Change	2010	https://www.ncbi.nlm.nih.gov/mesh/?term=Climate+Change
Clinical Protocols	1988	https://www.ncbi.nlm.nih.gov/mesh/?term=Clinical+Protocols
Conservation of Natural Resources	1977	https://www.ncbi.nlm.nih.gov/mesh/?term=Conservation+of+Natural+Resources
Cost Savings	1992	https://www.ncbi.nlm.nih.gov/mesh/?term=Cost+Savings
Costs and Cost Analysis	1966	https://www.ncbi.nlm.nih.gov/mesh/?term=Costs+and+Cost+Analysis
Culture	2024	https://www.ncbi.nlm.nih.gov/mesh/68003469
Economics, Medical	1999	https://www.ncbi.nlm.nih.gov/mesh/?term=Economics%2C+Medical
Education	1999	https://www.ncbi.nlm.nih.gov/mesh/68004493
Efficiency	1999	https://www.ncbi.nlm.nih.gov/mesh/68004526
Environmental Health	1999	https://www.ncbi.nlm.nih.gov/mesh/68004782
Environmental Pollution	1974	https://www.ncbi.nlm.nih.gov/mesh/68004787
Equipment and Supplies	1999	https://www.ncbi.nlm.nih.gov/mesh/68004864
General Practitioners	2011	https://www.ncbi.nlm.nih.gov/mesh/?term=General+Practitioners
General Surgery	2009	https://www.ncbi.nlm.nih.gov/mesh/68013502
Health Inequities	2022	https://www.ncbi.nlm.nih.gov/mesh/?term=Health+Inequities
Health Services Accessibility	1978	https://www.ncbi.nlm.nih.gov/mesh/?term=Health+Services+Accessibility
Home Care Services	1967	https://www.ncbi.nlm.nih.gov/mesh/68006699
Medical Overuse	2016	https://www.ncbi.nlm.nih.gov/mesh/?term=Medical+Overuse
Midwifery	1966	https://www.ncbi.nlm.nih.gov/mesh/?term=Midwifery
Nurses	1967	https://www.ncbi.nlm.nih.gov/mesh/68009726
Nursing	1999	https://www.ncbi.nlm.nih.gov/mesh/68009729
Nursing care	1966	https://www.ncbi.nlm.nih.gov/mesh/68009732
Nutritional Sciences	2007	https://www.ncbi.nlm.nih.gov/mesh/68052756
Nutritionists	2014	https://www.ncbi.nlm.nih.gov/mesh/?term=Nutritionists

(continued)

Table A.1 (continued)

MeSH Terms	Entry Date	URL
Organizational Innovation	1989	https://www.ncbi.nlm.nih.gov/mesh/?term=Organizational+Innovation
Patient Participation	1978	https://www.ncbi.nlm.nih.gov/mesh/?term=Patient+Participation
Perception	1999	https://www.ncbi.nlm.nih.gov/mesh/68010465
Pharmacists	1968	https://www.ncbi.nlm.nih.gov/mesh/68010595
Pharmacy	1999	https://www.ncbi.nlm.nih.gov/mesh/68010604
Physical Therapists	2012	https://www.ncbi.nlm.nih.gov/mesh/?term=physical+therapists
Physical Therapy Modalities	2006	https://www.ncbi.nlm.nih.gov/mesh/?term=physical+therapy+modalities
Physical Therapy Specialty	2012	https://www.ncbi.nlm.nih.gov/mesh/?term=physical+therapy+specialty
Physicians	1999	https://www.ncbi.nlm.nih.gov/mesh/68010820
Quality of Health Care	1968	https://www.ncbi.nlm.nih.gov/mesh/?term=Quality+of+Health+Care
Recycling	2011	https://www.ncbi.nlm.nih.gov/mesh/68059027
Social Determinants of Health	2014	https://www.ncbi.nlm.nih.gov/mesh/?term=Social+Determinants+of+Health
Social Justice	1978	https://www.ncbi.nlm.nih.gov/mesh/?term=Social+Justice
Technology	1999	https://www.ncbi.nlm.nih.gov/mesh/68013672
Telemedicine	1993	https://www.ncbi.nlm.nih.gov/mesh/?term=Telemedicine
Value-Based Purchasing	2013	https://www.ncbi.nlm.nih.gov/mesh/?term=Value-Based+Purchasing
Waste Management	1995	https://www.ncbi.nlm.nih.gov/mesh/?term=Waste+Management

Appendix B
Publications Per Sector

Decade	Building	Healthcare	Building
1940	1		
1960	3	1	1
1970	22	2	5
1980	8	4	3
1990	63	4	128
2000	1154	75	599
2010	4821	582	2267
2020	5551	2154	4595
Total	**11,623**	**2,822**	**7,598**

Source openalex

G. Brulé, *Reducing the Environmental Impact of Healthcare Systems*, Sustainable Business Development, https://doi.org/10.1007/978-3-032-34889-0

Appendix C
Material Footprint

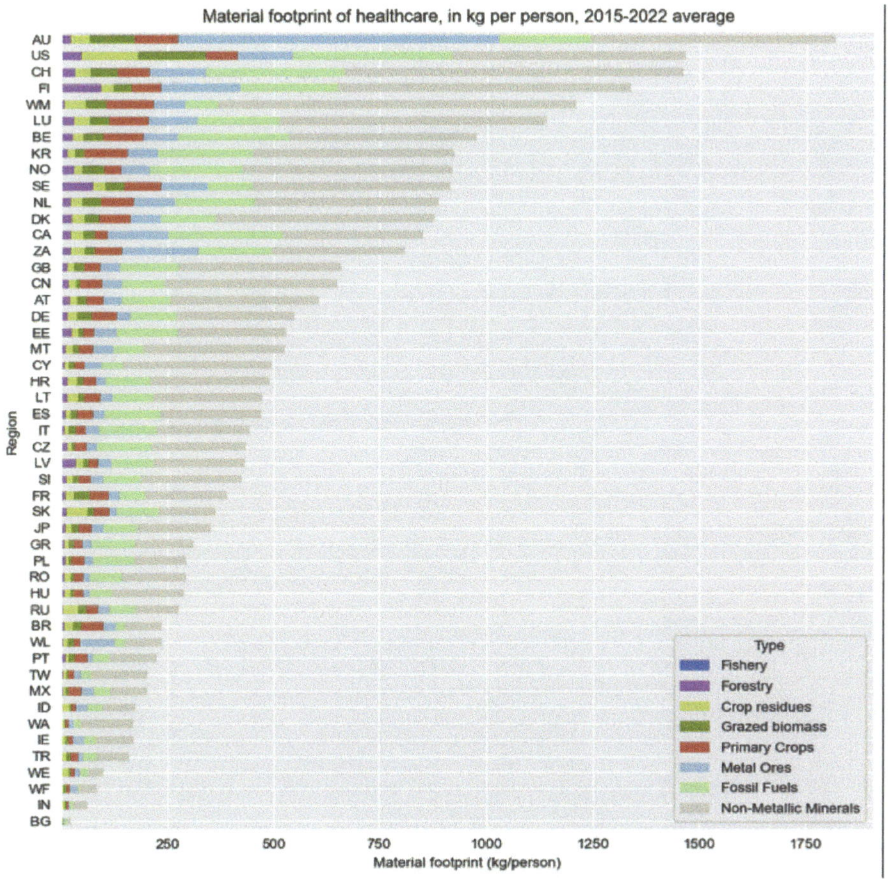

Credits: dr. Thomas Gibon

G. Brulé, *Reducing the Environmental Impact of Healthcare Systems*, Sustainable Business Development, https://doi.org/10.1007/978-3-032-34889-0

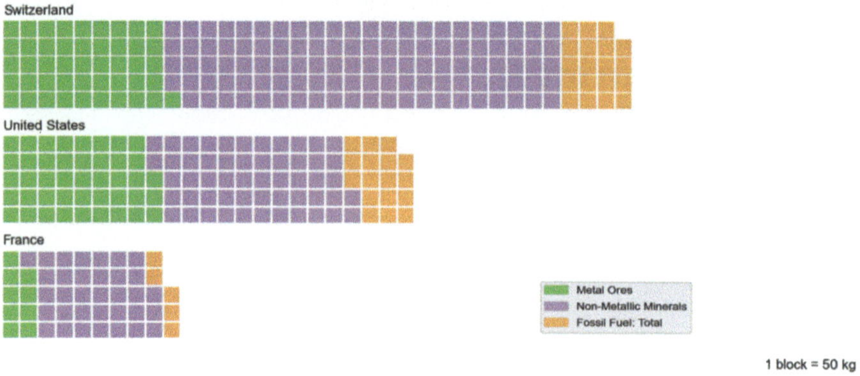
Switzerland
United States
France
Metal Ores
Non-Metallic Minerals
Fossil Fuel: Total
1 block = 50 kg

Appendix D
Metrics of Innovation

#	Metric name	Category	Environmental dimension	Primary source	Brief definition
1	Total R&D spending	Input	None	OECD Frascati Manual	Total expenditure on research and development
2	Green R&D budget allocation	Input	Explicit	OECD Green Growth	R&D budget specifically allocated to environmental innovation
3	Sustainable innovation programs	Input	Explicit	EU Horizon Europe	Number or funding of sustainability-focused innovation programs
4	Green procurement policies	Input	Explicit	OECD Public Procurement	Policies mandating environmental criteria in procurement
5	Environmental conditions in funding	Input	Explicit	EU funding frameworks	Funding mechanisms with environmental performance conditions
6	Innovation hubs, incubators	Input	None	OECD Innovation Policy	Number or capacity of innovation hubs and incubators
7	Sustainability-focused centers	Input	Explicit	Academic literature	Research centers dedicated to sustainability innovation
8	STEM graduates, researchers	Input	None	OECD S&T Indicators	Human capital in science, technology, engineering, mathematics
9	Sustainability training in health	Input	Explicit	WHO/academic programs	Training programs on sustainability for health professionals

(continued)

G. Brulé, *Reducing the Environmental Impact of Healthcare Systems*, Sustainable Business Development, https://doi.org/10.1007/978-3-032-34889-0

(continued)

#	Metric name	Category	Environmental dimension	Primary source	Brief definition
10	Clinical trials with sustainability endpoints	Process	Explicit	ClinicalTrials.gov	Clinical trials including environmental/ sustainability outcomes
11	Development cycle time	Process	None	OECD Oslo Manual	Time from concept to market launch
12	Commercialization time lag	Process	None	Academic literature	Delay between innovation creation and market entry
13	Collaboration intensity	Process	None	Bibliometric analysis	Degree of inter-organizational or cross-sector collaboration
14	Cross-sector partnerships	Process	Partial	OECD Innovation surveys	Number of partnerships across different sectors
15	Patent-paper linkages	Process	None	OECD STI Scoreboard	Citations from patents to scientific literature
16	Number of patents filed/granted	Output	None	OECD Oslo Manual	Total patents filed or granted in period
17	Green patents (IPC Y02)	Output	Explicit	OECD Green Growth Indicators	Patents in climate change mitigation technology classes (IPC Y02)
18	Patent environmental claims	Output	Partial	USPTO/EPO databases	Patents with environmental-related claims in

Appendix E
Frugal Innovation

Context	Frugal innovation	Elemental count (Frugal vs. Traditional)	Source
Insulin storage	Clay pot refrigeration (zeerpot)	5 elements (Si, O, Al, Fe, Ca - local clay) vs. more than 20 elements (Cu, Al, Fe, rare earths, refrigerants, polymers - global supply chains)	Traditional technology
Diagnostics	Portable ultrasound	circa 15 elements (simplified electronics, basic transducers) vs. more than 25 elements (advanced imaging chips, multiple transducers, high-resolution displays)	GE Healthcare
Dialysis access	Peritoneal dialysis	10–15 elements (dialysate solution, plastic catheter) vs. more than 25 elements (hemodialysis machine: pumps, filters, electronics, water treatment)	Deccan Hospital, India
Surgical repair	Mosquito net mesh for hernia repairs	5–8 elements (polyethylene mesh: C, H, O, N) vs. 15–20 elements (synthetic surgical mesh with metallic reinforcement components)	Ghana (Harris et al. 2018)
Diagnostics	Paper-based diagnostic tools	5 elements (cellulose, reagents: C, H, O, N, simple colorimetric indicators) vs. more than 20 elements (laboratory equipment with electronics, optics, reagents)	Multiple LMICs

G. Brulé, *Reducing the Environmental Impact of Healthcare Systems*, Sustainable Business Development, https://doi.org/10.1007/978-3-032-34889-0

Appendix F
Barriers to Implantation

Structural Barriers (Macro Level).

Although we explicitly said that the scope of the book was not macro, we list here the factors that influence the lack of accounting of environmental impacts. There are numerous: economic mis-incentives, policy gaps, supply chain lock-in, cultural paradigms and power struggles within the healthcare sector (conflicts of interest).

Economic Mis-Incentives

At the moment, this is limited by several factors, such as the structure of costs and benefits and the absence of a "polluter pays" principle in healthcare financing models. This principle emerged after the Minamata accident in 1956 showing direct and dramatic effects of mercury on health of the newborns on the island of Kyushu (Japan). Because most of the impacts of the healthcare system are less dramatic but more diffuse (as well as for the other sectors), the integration of the externalities is not yet on the agenda. While industrial facilities pay for emissions through carbon taxes or cap-and-trade systems, hospitals emit freely. The fee-for-service model entails that the more procedures performed, tests ordered, and medications prescribed, the greater the revenue, regardless of ecological consequences. This payment structure typically favors resource-intensive interventions over prevention, acute treatment over chronic disease management, hospital care instead of home care. Hospital purchasing departments optimize economicity and rentability of the care while true lifecycle costs (manufacturing emissions, transportation impacts, disposal burdens) remain largely invisible or are borne by other actors. The physician choosing pressurized metered-dose inhalers over dry powder alternatives faces no financial consequence for the 28 kg CO_2 differential per prescription, should he/she be even aware of this difference. Carbon emissions, toxic waste, resource depletion, and ecosystem degradation never appear on organizational balance sheets. There are little incentives

G. Brulé, *Reducing the Environmental Impact of Healthcare Systems*, Sustainable Business Development, https://doi.org/10.1007/978-3-032-34889-0

to invest in reusable materials unless the healthcare workers ask for it themselves. Unless environmental impact assessments become mandatory components of healthcare financing, economic incentives will continue rewarding practices that maximize throughput while externalizing ecological harm.

Policy and Regulatory Gaps

Healthcare operates within regulatory frameworks prioritizing patient safety, clinical quality, and infection control. Whereas laudable, these goals create environmental blind spots. The impacts in terms of global warming, ocean acidification, use of resource, water pollution are virtually absent. Everything happens as if environmental performance is optional. Most jurisdictions lack enforceable carbon reduction targets for healthcare institutions. While some countries have established net-zero commitments for health systems (e.g., NHS England's 2040 target), these remain aspirational rather than binding. Environmental reporting, where required, typically relies on voluntary frameworks without standardized methodologies, enabling greenwashing through positive narratives, cherry-picked indicators, and selective disclosure.

Supply Chain Lock-In

Healthcare supply chains exhibit profound path dependencies that resist transformation. Global medical device manufacturers achieve economies of scale through standardized, disposable products distributed via established logistics networks. Hospitals procurement faces limited alternatives: reusable equivalents may be unavailable, incompatible with existing infrastructure, or very expensive at small volumes, even when lifecycle analysis demonstrates long-term benefits. Pharmaceutical supply chains also present some forms of lock-in since active pharmaceutical ingredients are manufactured in facilities in Asia, packaged in single-use plastics, and transported worldwide.

Cultural Paradigms and Societal Expectations

There is an underlying assumption within dominant narratives that medical progress equates technological advancement. In the collective imaginary, "good healthcare" means access to cutting-edge equipment, pharmaceuticals, and interventions regardless of environmental footprint. The cultural paradigm of "more is better" drives systematic overtreatment and resource escalation. Defensive medicine practices, fear of litigation, and patient demands for "everything possible" push clinicians toward maximalist approaches even when evidence supports watchful waiting or conservative management. This cultural dynamic operates beyond individual psychology to shape institutional norms and professional standards that encode excess as best practice (Govindarajan & Ramamurti, 2013).

Organizational Barriers (Meso Level)

At the meso level, typical brakes to changes to reduce the environmental impacts are temporal architecture of urgency, siloed decision-making and resistance to change.

Temporal Architecture of Urgency

Modern healthcare systems operate under what we might call a *temporal architecture of urgency*, a structuring of time that prioritizes speed, throughput, and immediate availability over resource efficiency. When surgical teams face pressure to complete more procedures in less time, the choice between reusable and disposable instruments becomes predetermined by the logic of the system itself. These include increased use of disposable supplies to reduce cleaning time, deployment of single-use monitoring equipment to avoid maintenance delays, and preference for pre-packaged medications over bulk dispensing systems that require additional staff time. Packages of equipment are open even though they might not be necessary "in case" this would be needed. This architecture of time is reinforced by staff shortages and turnover, which creates a form of time poverty, a condition where the scarcity of personnel translates directly into compressed decision-making timeframes. This time poverty has systematic environmental consequence since routines are trapped in resource-intensive modes. This resource-intensive mode is decided not through hierarchy or common agreement but through what Foucault calls a *disciplinary power*, a direct normalization. This can also be demonstrated via the Job Demands-Resources model (Bakker & Demerouti, 2007). Healthcare professionals face intensifying job demands (patient loads, time pressures, administrative burdens) while lacking sufficient resources (adequate staffing, time buffers, environmental training). This imbalance transforms environmental consciousness into an additional demand. The organizational message is clear, though rarely explicit: environmental stewardship is at best a luxury for when "real work" is complete, a condition that rarely arrives in chronically under-resourced healthcare settings.

Organizational Silos and Fragmented Decision-Making

Healthcare organizations, like many modern institutions, operate through deeply entrenched functional silos. Clinical departments, administration, procurement each have their own logic, their own language. Sustainability, cross-cutting by "nature", fall into the gaps between these silos. This fragmentation means no single actor possesses both authority and knowledge to implement systemic change. Clinicians who recognize environmental harms lack procurement authority. Sustainability officers lack clinical credibility. Administrators face conflicting priorities from multiple stakeholders. Performance metrics focus on domain-specific outcomes (patient satisfaction, clinical quality indicators, financial margins, throughput efficiency) with environmental impact absent or relegated to voluntary reporting. If "what gets measured gets managed", sustainability remains peripheral to organizational priorities.

The Ambivalence of Guidelines

Healthcare organizations exhibit profound resistance to change, what Richman et al. (2013) "health sector exceptionalism", a term that depicts the tendency for healthcare organizations to be more resistant to change than other technology-sensitive industries. This institutional conservatism operates through multiple mechanisms. The first one is the importance of guidelines and protocols, through which "best practices" are encoded in daily routines, regardless of environmental consequences. Clinical practice guidelines have proliferated in recent years (one hospital reported biannually updating over 4,000 guidelines, creating what one quality manager described as "unsettling"). The bureaucratic apparatus meant to ensure quality inadvertently ossifies practice, making sustainable alternatives appear as deviations from standards rather than improvements. Healthcare workers experience "regulatory objectivity" (Cambrosio et al., 2006). This generates the paradox one nurse articulated: "We don't like the rules and still we keep seeking new ones". Sustainability becomes another checkbox rather than transformative principle. On top of this, organizational cultures develop shared normative assumptions about things "should be done", which can act as brakes to novelty. For instance, the shift toward disposables in the 1970s-1980s created a "disposable logic" now taken for granted by practitioners.

Different Roles/Power Dynamics

Power relations play crucial roles in mediating sustainability dynamics. Senior clinicians, despite holding expert and legitimate power, may find their authority to implement time-intensive sustainable practices undermined by managerial control over scheduling and resource allocation.

Professional/Individual Barriers (Micro Level)

Professional Training

Hospitals and healthcare workers have traditionally underestimated their ecological footprint, focusing narrowly on clinical missions while overlooking their roles as major resource consumers, employers, and waste producers (Ulhøi & Ulhøi, 2009). Medical education, already overcrowded with clinical content, has little space for environmental considerations except new movements (de Lucia et al. 2025). This creates what might be called "clinical tunnel vision", an intense focus on individual patient care that makes broader systems thinking difficult to develop. Academic medicine rewarded specialization and clinical research more than interdisciplinary environmental thinking, competition more than cooperation. New medical technologies are assumed beneficial if they improve clinical outcomes, not if they diminish environmental footprint. Although improving, environmental literacy remains largely marginal in most curricula. This training gap produces practitioners who can calculate medication dosages with precision but cannot estimate the carbon footprint of their clinical decisions.

Competing Priorities

The medical paradigm of "safety above all", where patient safety and clinical efficacy are primed above anything, constitutes a strong anchor from the cultural perspective. Following the Hippocratic principle of "first, do no harm", it seems that any consideration beyond immediate patient outcomes is seen as a potentially dangerous distraction. This *Health Sector Exceptionalism* (Richman et al., 2013) further reinforces this barrier: "For a variety of reasons, health care organizations are more resistant to change than other technology-sensitive industries. Accordingly, health providers have particular difficulty implementing the normally painful changes that have transformed other industries". This exceptionalism manifests as a professional conviction that healthcare's life-or-death stakes justify exemption from environmental accountability that applies to other sectors.

Professional Identities

The intermeshed trends to value specialization and mastery of technological tools lead to professional hierarchies within healthcare that systematically valorize technological sophistication over resource efficiency. Physicians specializing in high-tech interventions (cardiac surgery, interventional radiology, intensive care) occupy positions of greater prestige, symbolic capital, and economic reward than those practicing preventive medicine, primary care, or community health. This hierarchy is also valid for nurses (Longchamp et al., 2015). This means that sustainable alternatives (often simpler, lower-tech, more labor-intensive) face the risk to be perceived as a regression rather than an innovation. Advocating for reusability or questioning unnecessary treatments can be seen compromising modernity or practicing "cookbook medicine". Career advancement, research funding, and peer recognition flow toward those who adopt cutting-edge technologies, not those who optimize existing resources.

Cognitive Biases and Psychological Distance

Healthcare professionals may face systematic cognitive barriers that impede environmental action despite awareness. Psychological distance (Trope & Liberman, 2010) may seem aloof (future problem), spatially distant (global issue), socially removed (affects others), and hypothetically uncertain (probabilistic threat) compared to the immediate, tangible, concrete demands of patient care.

References

De Lucia, S., Furlan, L., Montano, N., Kherad, O., & EFIM Choosing Wisely Working Group. (2025). Choosing wisely and climate crisis: Reducing low-value care as a strategy to curb healthcare environmental impact. *Internal and Emergency Medicine*.https://doi.org/10.1007/s11739-025-04063-6

Harris, M., Bhatti, Y., Prime, M., Del Castillo, J., & Parston, G. (2018). Low-cost innovation in healthcare: What you find depends on where you look. *Journal of the Royal Society of Medicine, 111*(2), 47–50. https://doi.org/10.1177/0141076817738501

Longchamp, P., Toffel, K., Bühlmann, F., & Tawfik, A. (2015). De la sociologie de l'innovation à l'imagination sociologique. La théorie des champs à l'épreuve de la profession infirmière. *Cahiers de recherche sociologique*, (59–60), 135–156. https://doi.org/10.7202/1036790ar

Richman, B. D., Mitchell, W., & Schulman, K. A. (2013). Organizational innovation in health care. *Policy, 5*(7). https://hmpi.org/wp-content/uploads/2017/02/HMPI-Richman-Mitchell-Schulman-Organizational-Innovation-in-Healthcare.pdf

Trope, Y., & Liberman, N. (2010). Construal-level theory of psychological distance. *Psychological Review, 117*(2), 440.

Ulhøi, J. P., & Ulhøi, B. P. (2009). Beyond climate focus and disciplinary myopia. The roles and responsibilities of hospitals and healthcare professionals. *International Journal of Environmental Research and Public Health*, *6*(3), 1204–1214.

Glossary

Anthropocene A proposed geological epoch in which human activities significantly alter Earth's climate and ecosystems, shaping health and environmental conditions.

Antimicrobial Resistance The capacity of microorganisms to resist antimicrobial treatments, partly driven by environmental contamination and misuse of antibiotics.

Carbon Footprint The total greenhouse gas emissions attributable to an activity or system, expressed in CO_2 equivalents (CO_2e)

Circular Procurement Purchasing strategies that prioritize reuse, repairability, durability, and recyclability to reduce resource use and waste.

Clinical De-implementation The structured reduction of low-value or unnecessary medical practices to improve care quality and reduce resource consumption.

Critical Raw Materials Strategically important minerals and metals with high supply risk, often used in medical technologies.

Decarbonization The reduction of carbon intensity in energy systems and supply chains to mitigate climate change.

Deprescribing The supervised discontinuation or reduction of medications that are no longer beneficial or may be harmful.

Elemental Complexity The diversity of chemical elements in a product or device, influencing recyclability and material dependency.

Enhanced Recovery After Surgery Evidence-based perioperative protocols that shorten recovery time and reduce hospital resource use.

Frugal Innovation Resource-efficient solutions designed to deliver essential functions with minimal material and energy inputs.

Health Information Exchange Digital systems enabling secure sharing of patient data to reduce redundancy and improve efficiency.

Life Cycle Assessment A standardized method to evaluate environmental impacts across all stages of a product's life cycle.

Material Footprint The total mass of raw materials extracted globally to support a system's activities or consumption.

G. Brulé, *Reducing the Environmental Impact of Healthcare Systems*, Sustainable Business Development, https://doi.org/10.1007/978-3-032-34889-0

Operating Room Emissions Greenhouse gas emissions and material flows associated with surgical suites.

Paradigmatic Innovation A shift in underlying values and frameworks guiding healthcare organization and delivery.

Planetary Boundaries Biophysical thresholds that define a safe operating space for humanity within Earth systems.

Rebound Effect Increased consumption following efficiency gains, potentially offsetting environmental benefits.

Reverse Innovation An innovation developed in low-resource settings and later adopted in high-income contexts.

Scope 1 Emissions Direct greenhouse gas emissions from sources controlled by an organization.

Scope 2 Emissions Indirect emissions from purchased electricity, heating, or cooling.

Scope 3 Emissions Indirect emissions occurring along the value chain, including production and disposal.

Socio-Organizational Innovation Organizational or governance changes that improve sustainability without new technologies.

Sustainable Healthcare Healthcare delivery that improves health outcomes while minimizing environmental harm and resource depletion.

Technoproductive Innovation The development or adoption of new technologies or products in healthcare.

Technosphere The system of human-made infrastructures and technologies that transform resources and generate waste.

Technosphere-In Material and energy inputs entering the healthcare system.

Technosphere-Out Waste, emissions, and pollutants generated by healthcare activities.

Telemedicine Remote delivery of healthcare services using digital communication technologies.

Bibliography

Abbott, A. (1988). *The system of Professions*. Univ. Chicago Press.

Ahmad, S., Jaiswal, R., Yadav, R., & Verma, S. (2024). Recent advances in green chemistry approaches for pharmaceutical synthesis. *Sustainable Chemistry One World, 4*, Article 100029.

Aitken, H. G. J. (Ed.). (1965). Economic theory and entrepreneurial history. In *explorations in enterprise* (pp. 45–64). Harvard University Press. https://doi.org/10.4159/harvard.9780674594470.c5

Altıntaş, H., & Kassouri, Y. (2020). Is the environmental Kuznets Curve in Europe related to the per-capita ecological footprint or CO2 emissions? *Ecological Indicators, 113*, Article 106187. https://doi.org/10.1016/j.ecolind.2020.106187

Bakker, A. B., & Demerouti, E. (2007). The job demands-resources model: State of the art. *Journal of Managerial Psychology, 22*(3), 309–328.

Barrett, R. (2017). *The values-driven organization: Cultural health and employee well-being as a pathway to sustainable performance*. Taylor & Francis. https://books.google.fr/books?hl=fr&lr=&id=QjwlDwAAQBAJ&oi=fnd&pg=PP1&dq=swb+values+organization+alignment&ots=huskE2QUzK&sig=URgfuyUg2aiHJaUBAd3EJt9SC48

Berg, M. (1997). *Rationalizing medical work: Decision-support techniques and medical practices*. MIT press. https://books.google.fr/books?hl=fr&lr=&id=aOdG2TsVFiAC&oi=fnd&pg=PP15&dq=berg+rationalizing+medical+work&ots=bquKuo3Im-&sig=2AkB613fl9eweGBAkDODV7W6mC0

Bohigian, G. M. (1988). The golden age of medicine: 1966–1980. *Missouri Medicine, 85*(2), 71–74.

Bragan, J. H. (1979). *The Educational role of the church for a just and sustainable society*. Claremont School of Theology. https://search.proquest.com/openview/0808bf44c01d86c08755df46bd34bd85/1?pq-origsite=gscholar&cbl=18750&diss=y

Brulé, G., & Maggino, F. (2017). Towards More Complexity in Subjective Well-Being Studies. In G. Brulé & F. Maggino (Eds.), *Metrics of subjective well-being: limits and improvements* (pp. 1–17). Springer International Publishing. https://doi.org/10.1007/978-3-319-61810-4_1

Brulé, G., & Morgan, R. (2018). Working with stress: Can we turn distress into eustress. *Journal of Neuropsychology & Stress Management, 3*(4), 1–3.

Brulé, G., & Pichon, S. (2025). Promesses et défis de la télémédecine. *Revue Hospitalière de France* (Vol 625, pp.68–71).

Caron, F. (2010). La dynamique de l'innovation: Changement technique et changement social (XVIe-XXe siècle). *(No Title)*. https://cir.nii.ac.jp/crid/1130282272749144704

Castel, P. (2009). What's behind a guideline?: Authority, competition and collaboration in the French oncology sector. *Social Studies of Science, 39*(5), 743–764. https://doi.org/10.1177/0306312709104435

Commission, S. D. (2009). *NHS England carbon emissions carbon footprinting report*. https://research-repository.st-andrews.ac.uk/handle/10023/2377

G. Brulé, *Reducing the Environmental Impact of Healthcare Systems*, Sustainable Business Development, https://doi.org/10.1007/978-3-032-34889-0

Cosgrove, L., Krimsky, S., Wheeler, E. E., Peters, S. M., Brodt, M., & Shaughnessy, A. F. (2017). Conflict of interest policies and industry relationships of guideline development group members: A cross-sectional study of clinical practice guidelines for depression. *Accountability in Research, 24*(2), 99–115. https://doi.org/10.1080/08989621.2016.1251319

Daudey, J. (2023). *La pharmacie de Nietzsche: De la philosophie comme médecine*. https://www.torrossa.com/gs/resourceProxy?an=5509123&publisher=FZ2990

Davies, J. (2009). Clinical guidelines as a tool for legal liability. An international perspective. *Medicine and Law*. https://www.semanticscholar.org/paper/Clinical-guidelines-as-a-tool-for-legal-liability.-Davies/cb22608a776d4ce79fd6b2ba353a697596a3a42f

Simmons, J. C. (2003). Designing for quality:Hospitals look to the built environment to provide better patient care and outcomes. *The Quality Letter for Healthcare Leaders, 15*(4), 2–13, 1.

DiMaggio, P. (2013). Why cognitive (and cultural) sociology needs cognitive psychology. In *Culture in mind* (pp. 271–278). Routledge. https://api.taylorfrancis.com/content/chapters/edit/download?identifierName=doi&identifierValue=https://doi.org/10.4324/9780203904701-27&type=chapterpdf

Dunaiceva, J., Boillat-Blanco, N., Li, D., Niquille, A., Peytremann, A., Plüss-Suard, C., & Mueller, Y. (2025). Do Swiss family physicians prescribe antibiotics in line with national guidelines? A cross-sectional study. *Swiss Medical Weekly, 155*(6), 4234–4234. https://doi.org/10.57187/s.4234

Fernandez, A., Sturmberg, J., Lukersmith, S., Madden, R., Torkfar, G., Colagiuri, R., & Salvador-Carulla, L. (2015). Evidence-based medicine: Is it a bridge too far? *Health Research Policy and Systems, 13*(1), 66. https://doi.org/10.1186/s12961-015-0057-0

Gabbay, J., le May, A., Pope, C., Robert, G., Bate, P., & Elston, M.-A. (2011). Taking up the challenge: Local motives for the innovation. In *Organisational innovation in health services* (pp. 35–50). Policy Press. https://bristoluniversitypressdigital.com/abstract/book/9781847429391/ch003.xml

Geiselhart, K., Damm, M., Jeske, N., Knappmann, A., Nasser, G. P., Roth, L. F., Unkels, R., Winkler, A. S., Wolf, J., & Falkenberg, T. (2024). Sufficiency health-wise: Sustainable paths towards planetary and public health. *Frontiers in Public Health, 12*, 1497657. https://doi.org/10.3389/fpubh.2024.1497657

Gorman, E. H., & Sandefur, R. L. (2011). "Golden Age", quiescence, and revival: How the sociology of professions became the study of knowledge-based work. *Work and Occupations, 38*(3), 275–302. https://doi.org/10.1177/0730888411417565

Hocini, F. D., & Dallaporta, B. B. (2024). L'imagination aux sources de la création, dans le soin comme ailleurs. *Soins, 886*, 60–63.

Hussein, M., Pavlova, M., & Groot, W. (2023). An evaluation of the driving and restraining factors affecting the implementation of hospital accreditation standards: A force field analysis. *International Journal of Healthcare Management, 16*(2), 167–175.

Illich, I. (1974). *Energy and equity* (Vol. 6). Harper & Row. http://ww.w.ridemybike.org/energyandequity.pdf

Jithitikulchai, T., Feldhaus, I., Bauhoff, S., & Nagpal, S. (2021). Health equity funds as the pathway to universal coverage in Cambodia: Care seeking and financial risk protection. *Health Policy and Planning, 36*(1), 26–34.

Khan, A., Frazer-Green, L., Amin, R., Wolfe, L., Faulkner, G., Casey, K., Sharma, G., Selim, B., Zielinski, D., Aboussouan, L. S., McKim, D., & Gay, P. (2023). Respiratory management of patients with neuromuscular weakness: An American College of chest physicians clinical practice guideline and expert panel report. *Chest, 164*(2), 394–413. https://doi.org/10.1016/j.chest.2023.03.011

Kiefer, B. (2022). 14–Savoir environnemental et evidence-based medicine. *Santé et Environnement*. Retrieved March 8, 2026, from https://shs.cairn.info/article/MH_SENN_2022_01_0177/pdf

Klazinga, N., Lombarts, K., & van Everdingen, J. (1998). Quality management in medical specialties: The use of channels and dikes in improving health care in The Netherlands. *The Joint*

Commission Journal on Quality Improvement, 24(5), 240–250. https://doi.org/10.1016/S1070-3241(16)30378-9
Kumar, R. (2025). Bibliometric analysis: Comprehensive insights into tools, techniques, applications, and solutions for research excellence. *Spectrum of Engineering and Management Sciences, 3*(1), 45–62.
Lakoff, A. (2004). The Anxieties of globalization: Antidepressant sales and economic crisis in Argentina. *Social Studies of Science, 34*(2), 247–269. https://doi.org/10.1177/0306312704042624
Länsisalmi, H., Kivimäki, M., Aalto, P., & Ruoranen, R. (2006). Innovation in healthcare: A systematic review of recent research. *Nursing Science Quarterly, 19*(1), 66–72. https://doi.org/10.1177/0894318405284129
Lawrence, R., Capon, A., & Siri, J. (2017). Lessons from Hippocrates for contemporary urban health challenges. *Cities & Health, 1*(1), 72–82. https://doi.org/10.1080/23748834.2017.1372967
Lega, F., & De Pietro, C. (2005). Converging patterns in hospital organization: Beyond the professional bureaucracy. *Health Policy, 74*(3), 261–281.
Lovins, A. B. (1974). The case for long-term planning. *Bulletin of the Atomic Scientists, 30*(6), 38–50. https://doi.org/10.1080/00963402.1974.11458130
Malik, A., Lenzen, M., McAlister, S., & McGain, F. (2018). The carbon footprint of Australian health care. *The Lancet Planetary Health, 2*(1), e27–e35.
Michel, J. S., & Hargis, M. B. (2017). What motivates deviant behavior in the workplace? An examination of the mechanisms by which procedural injustice affects deviance. *Motivation and Emotion, 41*(1), 51–68.
Mol, A. (2006). Proving or improving: On health care research as a form of self-reflection. *Qualitative Health Research, 16*(3), 405–414. https://doi.org/10.1177/1049732305285856
Moon, J. C., & Bogle, R. G. (2006). Switching statins. *BMJ : British Medical Journal, 332*(7554), 1344–1345. https://doi.org/10.1136/bmj.332.7554.1344
Moon, J. C., Bogle, R. G., & Minas, R. (2007). Statins audit: Wrong question, wrong conclusions. *The Lancet, 369*(9562), 640.
Naylor, C., & Appleby, J. (2012). Sustainable health and social care. *London: Kings Fund*. https://forestradio.co.uk/A4W/Sustainable%20health%20and%20social%20care.pdf
Osterwalder, A., & Pigneur, Y. (2014). Business model generation. *Jakarta: Elex Media Komputindo*. https://cimne.com/cvdata/cntr2/spc2390/dtos/dcs/businessmodelgenerationpreview.pdf
Pel, B., Haxeltine, A., Avelino, F., Dumitru, A., Kemp, R., Bauler, T., Kunze, I., Dorland, J., Wittmayer, J., & Jørgensen, M. S. (2020). Towards a theory of transformative social innovation: A relational framework and 12 propositions. *Research Policy, 49*(8), Article 104080.
Pickles, K., Haas, R., Guppy, M., O'Connor, D. A., Pathirana, T., Barratt, A., & Buchbinder, R. (2024). Clinician and health service interventions to reduce the greenhouse gas emissions generated by healthcare: A systematic review. *BMJ Evidence-Based Medicine, 29*(5), 300–312.
Pinho-Gomes, A.-C., Yoo, S.-H., Allen, A., Maiden, H., Shah, K., & Toolan, M. (2022). Incorporating environmental and sustainability considerations into health technology assessment and clinical and public health guidelines: A scoping review. *International Journal of Technology Assessment in Health Care, 38*(1), Article e84. https://doi.org/10.1017/S0266462322003282
Porter, M. E. (2010). What Is Value in Health Care? *New England Journal of Medicine, 363*(26), 2477–2481. https://doi.org/10.1056/NEJMp1011024
Rosa, H. (2003). Social acceleration: Ethical and political consequences of a desynchronized high–speed society. *Constellations: An International Journal of Critical & Democratic Theory, 10*(1). https://www.academia.edu/download/114230322/social-acceleration.pdf
Roschnik, S., Martinez, G. S., Yglesias-Gonzalez, M., Pencheon, D., Tennison, I., & Organization, W. H. (2017). *Transitioning to environmentally sustainable health systems: The example of the NHS in England*. https://pesquisa.bvsalud.org/portal/resource/essiqueira/who-325309
Sackett, D. L., Rosenberg, W. M., Gray, J. M., Haynes, R. B., & Richardson, W. S. (1996). Evidence based medicine: What it is and what it isn't. In *Bmj* (Vol. 312, Issue 7023, pp. 71–72). British Medical Journal Publishing Group. https://www.bmj.com/content/312/7023/71?hwo

Seppänen, A.-V., & Or, Z. (2025). A scoping review of interventions to reduce the environmental footprint of healthcare. *Value in Health.* https://www.sciencedirect.com/science/article/pii/S1098301525000634

Shellian, B., & Levinson, W. (2016). When more is not always better: Choosing nursing interventions wisely. *Nursing Leadership (Toronto, Ont.), 29*(4), 8–9.

Shukla, V., Prashar, S., & Ramkumar, M. (2025). Investigating the potential of blockchain technology in enabling circular economy practices in Industry 5.0: An electronics industry case study. *Benchmarking: An International Journal.* https://www.emerald.com/insight/content/doi/https://doi.org/10.1108/BIJ-06-2024-0482/full/html

Sturmberg, J. P. (2019). Evidence-based medicine—Not a panacea for the problems of a complex adaptive world. *Journal of Evaluation in Clinical Practice, 25*(5), 706–716. https://doi.org/10.1111/jep.13122

Tess-IP. (2025, August 29). Recension - La pharmacie de Nietzsche: De la philosophie comme médecine. *Implications philosophiques.* https://www.implications-philosophiques.org/recension-la-pharmacie-de-nietzsche-de-la-philosophie-comme-medecine/

Thapa, D. R., Stengård, J., Ekström-Bergström, A., Areskoug, K., Krettek, A., & Nyberg, A. (2022). Job demands, job resources, and health outcomes among nursing professionals in private and public healthcare sectors in Sweden – a prospective study. *BMC Nursing, 21*(1), 140. https://doi.org/10.1186/s12912-022-00924-z

Timmermans, S. (2005). From autonomy to accountability: The role of clinical practice guidelines in professional power. *Perspectives in Biology and Medicine, 48*(4), 490–501. https://doi.org/10.1353/pbm.2005.0096

Udegbe, F. C., Ebulue, O. R., Ebulue, C. C., & Ekesiobi, C. S. (2024). The role of artificial intelligence in healthcare: A systematic review of applications and challenges. *International Medical Science Research Journal, 4*(4), 500–508.

Van Gendt, M., Ten Teije, A., Serban, R., & Van Harmelen, F. (2005). Formalising Medical Quality Indicators to Improve Guidelines. In S. Miksch, J. Hunter, & E. T. Keravnou (Eds.), *Artificial intelligence in medicine* (Vol. 3581, pp. 201–210). Springer Berlin. https://doi.org/10.1007/11527770_29

Vaughan, S., & Wells, R. (2025). *7988 5 Steps to reduce your carbon footprint for paediatric teams.* BMJ Publishing Group Ltd. https://adc.bmj.com/content/110/Suppl_1/A247.2.abstract

Wadmann, S., Holm-Petersen, C., & Levay, C. (2019). 'We don't like the rules and still we keep seeking new ones': The vicious circle of quality control in professional organizations. *Journal of Professions and Organization, 6*(1), 17–32. https://doi.org/10.1093/jpo/joy017

Zgardau, A., Hathi, K., Fowler, J., Mullowney, T., Price, A., Husein, M., Graham, M. E., Dzioba, A., Madou, E., & Strychowsky, J. E. (2024). Carbon footprint reduction associated with multidisciplinary Pediatric Airway Clinics: A program evaluation study. *OTO Open, 8*(3), Article e167. https://doi.org/10.1002/oto2.167

Zinsstag, J., Pelikan, K., Gonzalez, M. B., Kaiser-Grolimund, A., Crump, L., Mauti, S., Heitz-Tokpa, K., Bonfoh, B., Ali, S. M., & Abtidon, R. (2023). Value-added transdisciplinary One Health research and problem solving. In *Handbook of Transdisciplinarity: Global Perspectives* (pp. 333–350). Edward Elgar Publishing. https://www.elgaronline.com/edcollchap/book/9781802207835/book-part-9781802207835-31.xml

FSC
www.fsc.org
MIX
Papier | Fördert gute Waldnutzung
FSC® C083411

Kolibri 360 GmbH
Ferdinand-Jühlke-Straße 7
99095 Erfurt, Deutschland
produktsicherheit@kolibri360.de